Mastering Your Wellness Business©

Helping You Put the Pieces Together

By: Gail Sophia Edgell and Traci Brosman

What they are saying about

Mastering Your Wellness Business©

"While the title denotes this book will be useful in building a wellness business, the tips are outstanding and would be beneficial for anyone thinking of stepping into the world of creating their own company. When starting a new business/company, failure is not an option. The tips offered are pertinent guidelines to help ensure success and take eons off the learning curve."

Candace Booth, ND, PHD, CNC, SHC — Doctor of Naturopathy, Nutritionist & Spiritual Health Coach

"Gail Sophia Edgell and Traci Brosman are pioneers in assisting alternative doctors open up to their true potential as health care providers. Their no-nonsense advice is right on target. Too many alternative doctors give all to their patients, yet have little to show for their efforts financially. I thought I had heard it all; practice-building programs are rife throughout the chiropractic profession. Gail and Traci offer a fresh look at how to change the thinking process from one of negative thoughts to positive, from self-criticism to self-love."

Dr. Lani Simpson, D.C., C.C.D

"This book is the one place where you can get it all- it is not the usual marketing book for practitioners, but addresses the inner core principles skills required combined with cutting-edge relevant marketing techniques to build quickly a successful leveraged thriving business with clients you love."

Dr. Ann Lee, ND, Lac, Health for Life Clinic

"I loved the section on declaring myself to be the expert in my chosen field... and then creating events and media that support my niche...and only that niche. More than that, however, is the emphasis you placed on ACTION. I have been stuck many times in my career when 'thinking' about the next step I should take. Thinking actually interfered with progress. Once I finally decided to act, the challenge resolved itself in short order. Your pragmatic style and energetic approach to making a well care business a success is much appreciated here at Thrive Lancaster. It's refreshing to see someone with your 'Can Do' spirit helping health professionals help the masses."

Dr. Doug Meints, DC

"I know and respect Gail Edgell and Traci Brosman, They are creative, dedicated and most importantly sincerely conscientious in all areas of Holistic Mentoring. Together, they have the unique blend of caring, understanding and business savvy that I have grown to rely on. I regard them as a few of my trusted advisors. You should too!"

Ron Laker, CEO of NCS.tv and "C" Level Speaking

"Wellness professionals are often created out of passion for helping people. That passion doesn't always follow with or come with a plan. This book is a great guide for wellness professionals who want to make a living do what they love. It's comprehensive yet, not overwhelming. I love the integration of high-touch and high technology!"

MaryAnn Molloy, Chief Fun and Fitness Trainer, Healthy Body Fit Mind

"This book will motivate you with useful, practical information. It is the road map you need to speed along to achieving your professional and personal goals for your wellness business."

Julie Lusk, M.Ed., RYT, Wholesome Resources

"I spent 25 years in the banking world and worked most of those years as a commercial banker making loans to small businesses. The advice in this book is right on. Not only do Traci and Gail share a path to success for small business owners, they do it in an easy to read manor. I loved the personality of the book. This is a book you can't afford to miss!"

Jean Sumner, President, World Wellness Education

Copyright © 2012

Gail Sophia Edgell and Traci Brosman

FORWARD

It has been a lot of hard work and long hours, but the completion of this book was a dream of ours. We are passionate about assisting wellness professionals move from surviving to thriving in their businesses. We truly believe that integrative medicine is the paradigm of the future. The only way this can happen is to prepare holistic wellness professionals for the wave that is to come through creating successful business systems, effective marketing and mindset shifts.
Since the inception of Holistic Marketing Mentors, we have met so many dedicated professionals in various fields who are really making great strides with their clients and our goal is for them to share this with the world. We honor you for your dedication and service to others.

We are confident that this book, *Mastering Your Wellness Business* will give you valuable nuggets that will transform your business.

We are aware that there are mistakes in this book. Although, they are all unintentional we felt that it is more important to deliver this book to you as it is. We teach our clients that mistakes are normal and that they allow for opportunities for improvement. If we wait until everything is perfect than we will never complete anything because nothing is perfect. The ideas and resources in this book are invaluable and if you are one of the few individuals who are appalled when finding a mistake take a deep breath and relax. Keep reading and know that the content is much more important than any minor mistake.

ACKNOWLEDGEMENTS

We would like to thank our families for being so understanding during the writing and editing of this book and all the individuals who spent their time giving us valuable feedback, insights and testimonials. This includes Tony Edgell, Al and Heather Brosman, Cathy Vavrosky, Linda Hutt, Dr. Candace Booth, Sharon Brown, Ron Laker, Dr. Ann Lee, Julie Lusk, Dr. Doug Meints, MaryAnn Molley, Dr. Lani Simpson and Jean Sumner.

TABLE OF CONTENTS

Part 2 - Client Mastery   Page 70

C   CLIENTS Personality Types
L   LOVE Your Clients
I   IDEAL Customers
E   EVALUATING Clients
N   NOTEWORTHY Follow Ups
T   TAKING Care of Objections

Part 3 - Marketing Mastery   Page 111

M   MAGNIFICENT Videos
A   AWESOME Article and Blog
           Marketing
R   Your Customer's REAL Hot Buttons
K   KINETIC Newspaper, Magazines,
           Radio and TV
E   EVENTS: Sponsoring and Hosting
T   TAKING the Stage with Confidence
I   IMPACTFUL Social Media
N   NICHE Marketing
G   GENIUS Business Cards and
           Networking

Part 4 – Self Mastery   Page 174

M   The Successful MINDSET

A   Be AUTHENTIC, Be Real

S   STOPPING Limiting Beliefs and Self
Sabotage

T   THANKFULNESS

E   EXECUTING the Law of Attraction

R   REMOVING Feelings of Being
Overwhelmed

Y   YOU, Everyday Self Care

INTRODUCTION

We have all heard the story I got into this field because I wanted to help people or I started this business because I had an interest in health and wellness. They are both fabulous reasons, but let's be realistic - when it comes to business neither of them are going to keep the money coming in day after day.

Yes, we know you want to help people. You must understand though that it is perfectly okay to make a great living doing it. So many wellness professionals actually feel bad charging for their services. Sometimes they charge for one hour when they worked two or never even ask for a payment. Have you ever done this? Come on fess up!

Stop undervaluing yourself; stop devaluing your services and your clients healing process.

If you learn nothing else from this book, it is this: **you are a gift to this world. You know more than 95% of the people walking this planet in the area of health and wellness.** You are doing a disservice not only to yourself, but also to those that you are helping when you do not charge what your services are worth.

You might think another certification or degree is going to send you through the roof of success. Here is the truth though...it is a waste of your time if you do not also have the business skills in place to implement what you know. Do not spend another dime until you sit down and have a long talk with yourself about where your business is going and why it is not where you thought it would be.

If you are just starting out, give yourself a big pat on the back because you are already making some great business decisions. This book will take years off your learning curve and is your shortcut to success.

This book is written to help you succeed with your business. Take it to heart. All of the strategies in this book are things successful entrepreneurs have utilized over the years to take their business to the next level.

Success looks different for everyone. Choose what resonates with you. Most important...commit to making a change.

Take action steps. Yep, you are going to have to do some things. This is not the book, _The Secret_, where things manifest if you think about them.

Schedule the action items in your planner and do them!

NO MORE procrastinating. Don't read this book like every other book you have picked up and chosen not to take action with. We have made it easy; take it one-step at a time to grow your business to where you want it to go.

Be the healer, coach, trainer you were designed to be.

Having a successful business is similar to putting together the pieces of a puzzle. If you have all the pieces together, your business flows with ease. But, if you are missing pieces along the way, your business seems fragmented and takes lots of effort on a daily basis, which will eventually lead to burn out.

This book is designed to help you in the following main areas:

Business Mastery
Client Mastery
Marketing Mastery
Self Mastery

Just like the puzzle, you must have all of these in place to truly find success.

You will find exactly what you need in this book to bring your business to that next level of success.

Here, you are getting all of the pieces to the puzzle.

For each mastery piece, you will discover:

What it is

Why it is important for your business

How to implement it

Action steps you can take

Additional resources to make implementation that much easier

To Your Success!
Gail & Traci

BUSINESS MASTERY

Being in business is a serious matter; you may have thought that working for yourself was going to be much easier than working for someone else. You soon find out that it is just another job with a lot more responsibility. In fact, you worked less hours and probably made more money per hour when you worked for someone else.

You may start to question, did I make the right choice and is this really worth it?

Yes, being in business for yourself is extremely rewarding and yes, it can provide you with flexibility. But it can also be a lot of hard work and there is always an energy exchange. In the beginning when you do not have a lot of money you sacrifice more of your time. As your success grows, you outsource more spending more money to gain more time.

BUSINESS MASTERY TIP #1

BUSINESS Entity Structure, Financial Team and Outsourcing/Employees

Why does the type of business structure you choose have anything to do with success? Time and time again, individuals do not take the time to meet with a lawyer and/or accountant when setting up their business and in the end give thousands of dollars to the IRS at tax time. Do not go down this road. It can be a very UGLY path!

> *Sheri's Story - Sheri is a holistic practitioner who went into business for herself and made an extremely nice income her first year. All was well and good until April 15th when Sheri had to pay a huge income tax bill and had no idea that it was coming. She actually had to take out a bank loan to pay off the IRS. In the end, Sheri could have saved herself a lot of money just by taking the time to seek professional advice.*

If you do not think you can afford advice, than check out do it yourself legal services such as Legal Zoom, Nolo or Rocket Lawyer. They will at least lead you in the right direction. Deciding whether or not you should be a sole proprietor, LLC, S corporation or a C corporation can be confusing. For most businesses "S" corporations are sufficient, but if you intend to raise capital, a "C" corporation may be appropriate. Again, seek professional advice.

You may also want to look at obtaining liability and malpractice insurance. We have included several companies where you can get quotes from in the Additional Resources section.

Make sure your accounting books start clean and stay clean. The worst thing you can do is start mixing business and pleasure. It creates a nightmare for you and your accountant.

How do you choose your business entity structure and financial team?

Contact an attorney or Legal Zoom and make sure you ask lots of questions so you can make the best choice for you. Questions such as:

> What paperwork needs to be filed to establish your corporation?

> How much does it cost to set up the corporation?

> What paperwork is required annually?

> How much does it cost to file your annual paperwork?

> What are you required to do? (Annual meeting of shareholders, minutes of meetings, etc.)

How are business and personal assets protected in case of a lawsuit?

How will your business entity choice affect your year-end taxes?

Ask your accountant how your financial books should be set up for tax purposes.

Hire a bookkeeper to help you set up everything in your checking account and your accounting procedures. Get a bookkeeper and accountant that have experience with your type of business, understand your states laws and be clear on what you need at fiscal year-end. Make sure you also ask for references.

You will want to choose someone who can guide you with financial decisions and explain the numbers to you on a regular basis. If your bookkeeper cannot do this then make sure you are consulting with your accountant regularly. Accounting is not just entering your receipts, paying your expenses and filing your taxes. It is important to understand your financial status at all times. Your bookkeeper and accountant are key partners in your success.

When do you decide to outsource or hire employees?

When you first start out in business, you might think that you cannot afford to have employees. This may be true. However, one of the biggest mistakes business owners make is working in their business instead of on their business. There will come a point when you need to ask yourself, am I losing money because I do not have someone to help me? Instead of thinking, how long can I wait before I hire help? Ask the question, how soon can I get my business to a point where I can hire someone to help me take it to the next level?

How do you choose to hire employees or outsource?

The traditional way of getting help in your business is to hire independent contractors or employees. Be sure to check with your accountant regarding laws and added expenses such as taxes, liability and insurance. Typically, you will hire an employee for a certain number of hours per week and they will do a wide variety of tasks. You might want to hire an independent contractor for specific, ongoing tasks. Independent contractors are responsible for setting their hours, deciding how they complete the tasks, and they usually provide all of their own equipment and supplies.

Another great hiring option is outsourcing. Outsourcing is contracting someone to help with tasks that are ongoing or one-time projects. You hire them as an independent contractor. They may work for themselves or for someone else. Outsourced help can answer your phones, check and respond to your emails, follow up with your clients, send out newsletters, assist with social media marketing, etc.

Questions you should ask yourself on a regular basis are can this task be done by someone other than me? If I could have someone else do this task, could I be seeing more clients or bringing in additional income into my business? If the answer is yes to both these questions, than outsource.

Another reason to outsource is if you really dislike doing a particular task. This will create resistance and negativity in your business. So take it off of your to do list and hire someone else to do it.

We have included many outsourcing options in the Additional Resources section below.

Many of these relationships end up being like marriages, so be sure you mesh with the person. Ask around and see whom others are using. When outsourcing any task be specific with the person doing the work on how you want it done, how long it should take and when you expect it to be completed. You may find that doing a quick tutorial is very helpful. You can easily create quick tutorials using video software like Camtasia or Jing. Test the waters by giving them something small to do and evaluate how they complete the task.

Last, request an update on a daily basis as to what they have completed. This way everyone is on the same page and you have fewer problems due to lack of communication.

What are some key actions steps you can take?

Research what business structure is appropriate for your business.

Hire someone to help you with your bookkeeping and accounting needs. You may be able to find an accountant that has a bookkeeper on staff.

Determine how much your time is worth. Brainstorm tasks that you may want to outsource or hire independent contractors or employees.

Prioritize this list.

Get outsourcing quotes for the top two priority tasks. This way you know how much it will cost you to have someone do these for you.

Resources

4 Hour Work Week by Timothy Ferriss
www.legalzoom.com – Legal entity advice and structuring
www.rocketlawyer.com – Legal entity advice and structuring
www.nolo.com– Legal entity advice and structuring
www.ssbaccounting.com – Accounting and bookkeeping service
www.presidioinsurance.com - Insurance services
www.dropbox.com – Sharing of files
www.vworker.com - Virtual assistants
www.asksunday.com - Virtual assistants
www.b2kcorp.com - Virtual assistants
www.taskseveryday.com – Virtual assistants; must hire 20 to 40 hours per week
www.elance.com – Project outsourcing; post your project and receive bids
www.fiverr.com – Project outsourcing; all tasks for $5.00
www.techsmith.com/camtasia – Video, webinar and audio editing software
www.techsmith.com/jing - Record short tutorials
www.join.me - Share screen and collaborate live

BUSINESS MASTERY TIP #2

UNIQUE Partnerships, Affiliates and Masterminds

UNIQUE Partnerships

Unique partnerships, affiliates and mastermind groups are the fastest ways to grow your business and they are a win-win for everyone.

Unique partnerships are created when you find someone or a business that complements your business. For instance, if you specialize in treating clients or clients with allergies you might consider partnering with someone who does flooring or air filtrations systems. People with allergies often have to replace carpets with flooring and may need to filter the air in their home. When creating partnerships with these types of businesses, you can actively refer your customers and vice versa. Everyone wins including the client.

Never limit your ideas of businesses or people that might make great partnerships. It never hurts to ask. If you do not ask, you will never know and the answer will always be NO. If you ask, you might get a MAYBE or even a YES.

Don't forget to approach your peers. Just remember to play nice in the sandbox. We encourage cooperation with your peers instead of competition.

You might have six other naturopaths, personal trainers, chiropractors or acupuncturists in your immediate area, but most likely, you will be targeting a different type of client. Look for ways you can mutually benefit from each other. Customers love it when professionals play nice together. This creates an immediate factor of trust, both among your peers and among your clients. If you are confident in your abilities you don't have to worry about anyone taking clients or ideas from you.

UNIQUE Affiliates

Affiliates are another form of referral. This term is used heavily in the Internet marketing world. Some Internet marketers feel this part of the industry has gotten out of hand, because some people are promoting everything and anything, even if they do not believe in it.

You want to be authentic and only promote products and services that you believe in and find people that will do the same for you.

Setting up to work with affiliates is a little more involved and you may find it easier to outsource the set-up to someone else rather than do it yourself. Don't let the time involved stop you though. This is a great way to build a strong referral network if you are generating income from online sources. This is also an excellent tool if your partners will be sending their leads emails or using social media to promote you AND if your clients can make purchases or book appointments online.

Affiliate programs track who made the referral and any purchases and/or appointments that resulted from the referral. They can track future purchases as well and give detailed reports for you and your affiliates. Check out the additional resource section for a few affiliate-tracking programs.

UNIQUE Masterminds (also known as Professional Roundtables)

Mastermind groups can be magical. In fact, it is a little known fact, that as of the writing of this book we (Gail & Traci) have never met. That's right...we have written two books together, launched a successful consulting and group coaching business, Holistic Marketing Mentors, and yet we have never met face-to-face. We were introduced by the way of a mastermind group in February of 2010. There were six people in the mastermind group for nearly two years. All of us contributed to each other's businesses in ways that were absolutely priceless, forming life-long relationships and partnerships that have had an outstanding effect on each of our businesses.

The brainstorming and advice that comes from sharing strategies with other like-minded business people can take your business to the next level quicker than anything else you do for your business. This is why some mastermind groups charge six figures just to be involved. A new entrepreneur can rarely afford this type of expense. Do not get discouraged because you can still find excellent mastermind groups for less than what you pay for one meal eating out. If you want to give masterminding a try, check out ours in the Additional Resources section below. We keep our mastermind groups small and affordable so that every individual gets the help they need.

What are some key actions steps you can take?

Make a list of unique partnerships.

Make a list of peers (competitors).

Make appointments each week to connect with someone new and find out how you can support each other.

Set up a system to track your referrals.

Join a mastermind group.

Additional Resources

www.paygear.com - Affiliate programs
www.membersgear.com - Affiliate programs
www.1shoppingcart.com - Affiliate programs
www.easywebautomation.com - Affiliate programs
www.holisticmarketingmentors.com/mastermindgroup - Mastermind groups

BUSINESS MASTERY TIP #3

SUCCESSFUL Time Management

How many times have you heard someone say there is not enough time in the day? You have a lot of pressure with regard to your time - business, clients, friends, family and social activities are just a few. You may also belong to organizations that will help you market your business or learn new skills. This all takes additional time. It is easy to get overwhelmed and feel that there is not enough time to do it all.

Time is finite; there are only 24 hours in each day. However, if used well you can achieve many incredible accomplishments in these 24 hours.

The key to successful time management is to plan, prioritize and schedule. You may find it difficult to do everything on your to do list. However, most people can accomplish a lot more than they believe they can.

There is a saying, if you want to get something done then ask a busy person. Busy people know how to manage their time.

How do you manage your time successfully?

Before you can plan, you must get organized. People waste valuable time going from one task to another or looking for things they have lost.

One of the best tools to get organized is a software app called Evernote. This free app allows you to organize and categorize all of your notes in one location. You can immediately synchronize your notes with your phone or any computer, Kindle, etc. and share notes with other people. Best of all you can record your notes with your phones voice recorder or camera.

By typing in all of your notes in one place, you will no longer have to search for that sticky note that is always disappearing. Start by getting organized first thing every morning.

Benjamin Franklin said, "If you fail to plan, you plan to fail." Now that you have all your notes in one place it is time to plan and prioritize. Try using the to do lists app by Get it Done. You can try this free for 15 days and then after that it is $39.00 per year. There are also completely free to do lists such as Keep and Share, Google tasks and Outlook tasks, but Get it Done is much more flexible. You can tag tasks, have multiple lists, organize them by project, set up recurring tasks, send tasks to your to do lists by forwarding emails, and assign someone else the task.

Prioritizing is important. It is too easy to have your day become filled with menial tasks that will not bring you more clients or money. Pareto's Law says that 80% of your results are derived from only 20% of the tasks, products, clients and effort you produce. You want to identify which 20% of your daily tasks generate income for your business and do more of these and less of the others.

Every day make sure that you are doing something that will attract AND retain more clients and increase your income. These are your number one priorities, before answering and opening your email. Before you go through mundane paperwork, you must ask yourself does this task fulfill one of my top three daily priorities? Once you have completed one or two things that attract clients and increase your overall income then you can do all of the other things that will fill your day.

In addition, reduce the time you spend on non-important tasks. Parkinson's Law tells us that work expands according to how much time you have for its completion. If you have one hour, it will take one hour; if you allow only 10 minutes, it will only take 10 minutes.

Look for time suckers. Email and Facebook are probably high on many people's time sucking lists.

Tim Ferris from the *4 Hour Work Week* recommends looking at emails only once per day. If this seems impossible to you, try only checking email at certain times in your day such as 8 am, 1 pm and 4 pm.

Attention all email saving junkies. Yes, the following tip is directly aimed at your inbox that has hundreds or even thousands of emails. Ugh!

When you look at your emails, immediately respond or do what is needed, delegate someone else to do it or put the email in the trash. If it is something that you would like to read for further education later, put it in a file folder designated for this purpose. At the end of each week, delete everything in the "education" file. If you did not get to it this week, you are not going to get to it next week either. Purge it from your life.

Your goal is to have an email box with less than 10 items in it at all times.

Do not procrastinate. Procrastination causes worry and worry causes failure. When you worry, you are priming your brain to find more of it. Whatever you focus on the most in your life will become your life. So stop worrying about it and just schedule it and do it.

The final key to good time management is often the most difficult for people. You need to schedule when you are going to work on something and then you need to do it. Try using the calendar in Outlook and Google for this. You can share Google calendar with others and it will automatically synchronize with your Outlook and/or Google calendars on your computer and your phone.

There are also ways you can find additional time in your schedule. For instance, replace the time you spend watching television with something you need to do. If you are looking to find time to read or learn something new, try audio books. You can listen to these while you drive, clean house, workout or while you get ready for the day.

By developing excellent time management skills, you will reduce your stress levels because you will no longer worry that you forgot something or do not have enough time to get things done. You will get a lot more accomplished which will give you a sense of pride and make you feel good. You will feel successful and therefore you will be successful.

What are some action steps you can take?

Plan your tasks and projects for the year.

Break these down into smaller monthly, weekly, and daily tasks.

For recurring projects, set up recurring tasks immediately in your planner– this will save you time and will help you be consistent.

Prioritize your daily tasks and do at least two items that will attract new clients, retain current clients and increase your income.

Schedule all of these tasks on a calendar or in a to do list software application.

Additional Resources

www.evernote.com – Organizing
www.mindjet.com – Organizing
www.microsoftstore.com – To do lists, email management and scheduling
www.getitdoneapp.com – To do lists
www.keepandshare.com - To do lists
mail.google.com/mail/help/tasks - To do lists
www.google.com/calendar - Scheduling
www.doodle.com – Scheduling
www.timedriver.com - Scheduling

BUSINESS MASTERY TIP #4

IGNITE Your Programs:
Group and Corporate Wellness

IGNITE Your Group Programs

Go for the MANY! If you have a desire to make more money and help more people, group programs are one of your best options. For some reason, many people just focus on working with individuals, one-on-one. You tell each client the same thing over and over again, so why not make it into a group program? Group programs could be live classes, teleclasses, webinars, workshops, demonstrations, etc.

You might be saying, but I put my physical hands on people, how can I possibly offer a group program? Start by thinking outside the box. What about training people to do basic home techniques or combining it with lectures on nutrition, weight loss, chronic pain, etc.? What about workshops on prevention or even on maintaining wellness after sickness? Remember, ailments and diseases are not just one-sided. The best thing about all of this is that if you do not feel qualified to teach a section of the program, you can partner with someone to help you. Your partners can then advertise to their clients/customers. It is a win-win for all involved.

This is where a niche comes in handy. For example, a Naturopath could do a series on infertility, allergies or ADHD and have a guest speaker that specializes in exercise, detox, nutrition, etc. Do you get how easy it is to offer great programs?

You may want to put your programs online. This is not nearly as hard as people think, especially if you are offering group programs already. It is a matter of purchasing some basic equipment to video and audio tape your classes and a software program to edit everything. See the Additional Resources section for easy-to-use software and equipment that will make this task simpler for you.

If the editing portion is too overwhelming, outsource it. Most teenagers are very well versed at working with these programs and will jump at the chance to make some extra money.

You can also have everything transcribed, which can be sold as part of an online program. Best of all, when you speak at events and for organizations and clubs you will now have products that you can display at the back of the room to sell.

Think smart. The people that seem to have everything are just re-packaging their content. You can do the same and have multiple revenue streams.

How do you create impressive group programs and products?

It is a matter of committing the time to design the program and getting it out there to the world. Once it is completed, you can test it, make adjustments and offer it again. After that, it is just a matter of fine-tuning. Ask any entrepreneur about their current offerings. You will find that they have changed their program(s) over time with feedback and additional knowledge. Feedback is a wonderful thing. Do not take it personally. Make the necessary changes and aim to develop a better program.

This brings us to evaluations. In order to have effective programs you must evaluate them. This is the only way you can make changes. Evaluations should be completed immediately after the program, but also again, at three, six or nine months down the road. Do not be afraid to find out what needs improvement and what it will take to make your program REALLY successful.

If you are not quite sure of the contents of a program or what results might be seen by the participants, offer a pilot study. This gives you a chance to sort things out during the program and people can attend the program at a discounted rate. These attendees will gladly give you valuable feedback of what to delete, add, etc. They may even tell you that the program is terrible. Do not worry. If this is the case, you want to hear it quickly before you spend a lot of time and effort in the marketing stage.

Treat pilot studies just as if you were offering the real deal. Nothing is different other than the fact you are up front with the people you are inviting that this is a brand new program and it may have a few kinks that will need to be worked out. You will also only market to those in your immediate reach, email, current clients, potential clients, Facebook, Twitter, etc.

If you want to get technical with your pilot studies and even your regular programs, you may want to do pre- and post- measurements, which will help you in marketing your program in the future.

What are some key actions steps you can take?

You have many things to think about. One of the easiest things you can do is go to a park, sit quietly, and journal your initial thoughts about what your program might look like.

Determine whether a pilot program would be beneficial to you.

Determine a topic and start planning the basics.

How many weeks will the program be?

What will the dates and times be?

How will you deliver the program and where?

Who will your partners be?

What will everyone do for the program?

What results do you expect your clients to have?

How will you encourage them to stick through the entire program?

How much will you charge?

What will be offered at the end?

Plan the additional program details when you actually have people signed up for the program.

If you are still unsure of what to do, we will walk you through the process, step-by-step and give you easy to follow templates in the *How to Design and Implement a Kick Butt Program.* We guarantee that you get your group program off to the right start. See the Additional Resources section.

> *Gail's Story – For years I worked in corporate wellness and the most successful programs were those*

structured as friendly competitions. The
memory of this is when I worked at a corpc
as part of their annual employee picnic included
health and fitness activities. Employees were divided
into teams. Each team would strategize months
ahead of the picnic what employees were doing what
activities. In the end, the team that had the most
points got a silly trophy to display in the cafeteria.
Yes, this is all they received. People to this day walk
up to me in public and say, remember when we used
to have.... That is how much of an impact this
particular program/event had on their lives.
Employees had so much fun and as a result morale
improved in the corporation.

Additional Resources

www.holisticmarketingmentors.com/programdesign
- How to Design & Implement Kick Butt Programs
www.hotrecorder.com – Recorder
www.jingproject.com – Free short screencast
recorder
www.copytalk.com – Transcription services
www.voice2note.com – Transcribes voice notes into
Evernote
www.techsmith.com/camtasia – Video, webinar and
audio editing software
www.freeconferencing.com – Free conference calls,
teleseminars
www.anymeeting.com – Webinars
www.gotomeeting.com – Webinars
www.evergreenbusinesssystems.com – Webinars

www.linkedin.com – Network with business professionals, find key player who are brokers and in the insurance industry

www.referenceusa.com – You will need a library card to access and may need to go through your library's website for complete access

IGNITE Your Corporate Wellness Programs

Working in corporations is a great way to not only gain exposure, but also grow your business. Most professionals are afraid to even step in this territory and it is wide open. The reason this is scary for so many is they do not know where to begin.

How do you gain access to corporations?

One of the easiest ways is to access health insurance brokers. These brokers already have relationships with key decision makers in the corporations you want to target and if they like you, they can get you in the door quickly. Another option is to find key players in these organizations and speak to them or offer to help them at a discounted rate. Many times these are your best advocates.

Many times in your network of friends, there are individuals who know someone who can help you. If not in your immediate network, check your LinkedIn connections. Be clear on your objectives and goals before speaking to them. Check your local library to narrow down the businesses you are looking for by size and industry. You will also be able to often find contact information along with phone numbers and emails.

So many things can be offered in a corporate setting. Start with where you are comfortable and

ays expand. Here are some things you
can offer:

Group programs – one-time or a series.

One-on-one programs – especially to the management team.

Friendly competitions among staff or departments.

Yearly wellness program planning.

Monthly or quarterly wellness committee meetings.

Measure the success and outcomes of programs and wellness initiative.

Do all of their wellness programming and find the contractors to assist you.

What are some key actions steps you can take?

Put together an outline of your ideal corporate wellness program.

Contact potential partners.

Build relationships with several health brokers.

Determine the corporations you want to approach.

Additional Resources

www.linkedin.com – Network with business professionals, find key players who are brokers and in the insurance industry
www.referenceusa.com – You will need a library card to access and may need to go through your library's website for complete access

BUSINESS MASTERY TIP #5

NECESSARY Associations

Belonging to one of your industry associations can provide you with many benefits. It has been said that 85% of all failures in business occurred in businesses that did not belong to an association in their industry.

There are many reasons to join associations: group insurance, assistance with business problems, learning from your peers, staying on top of industry news and low-cost education. Remember, associations are the voice of your industry.

However, as with many things in life, you will only receive benefits equal to what you put into it. Before you begin even looking at associations, you need to decide what it is you hope to gain from them.

Networking groups are also invaluable to creating relationships with other professionals. Used correctly, you will find many ways to partner and refer amongst a large group of individuals.

How do you determine the associations you should belong to?

First and foremost, decide what you want the association to provide you. Then talk to others in your industry and find out where they belong. Find networking associations where you do not have to commit to a full year. That way if you do not like them, you can always terminate your membership. Sometimes associations will offer a trial period. This way you can test whether it is a good fit for you. The key is to participate during the trial period and not just join and do nothing.

What are some key actions steps you can take?

Find out from your local library or from a S.C.O.R.E. representative what associations may be applicable to your business.

Make a list of what you want to get out of the associations you join.

Write an email to send to all of your friends in the industry asking what associations they belong to and if they are getting value out of them.

Find out from the person recruiting you to the association what it takes to get the most out of you membership.

Decide if you can commit to doing what it takes to be successful within the association. If not, do not waste your time or money.

Commit to joining one association in the next two months.

Additional Resources

www.publiclibraries.com - Public Library Directory
www.score.org - Score Directory
www.uschamber.com – Chamber of Commerce Directory
www.networkingforprofessionals.com – Networking for Professionals
www.bni.com – Business Network International
www.tangerinenetworkinggroup.com – Tangerine Networking Group
www.woamtec.com – Women On a Mission to Earn Commission
www.nafe.com – National Association of Female Executives
www.wen-usa.com – Women's Entrepreneur Network
www.ewomennetwork.com – E-Women Network

BUSINESS MASTERY TIP #6

Becoming the EXPERT, Branding You

How do you differentiate yourself from all of your peers? How do you ensure your clients choose to do business with you rather than someone else down the street or even someone globally? You do this by branding yourself as the expert. Becoming the expert is essential to the overall success of your business.

Before we talk about how to become the expert, we must talk about why you are already the expert. As we said earlier in this book, you know more about your field than 95% of people who are not in your field. This automatically qualifies you as the expert. Being the expert DOES NOT mean that you know everything. Being the expert DOES NOT mean that you know more than anyone else on the subject does. Being the expert DOES MEAN that you have researched, studied and successfully put into practice the things you claim to be an expert in. Being an expert DOES MEAN that you continue to stay on top of new information in your field and that you always strive to give the very best possible advice to your clients. Being an expert also means admitting you do not know everything and being willing to find the answers when needed.

Think of Dr. Oz. Who exactly made him an expert in nutrition, exercise, supplements, weight loss, and chronic fatigue syndrome? He did or you might even say Oprah did. Dr. Oz by trade is a cardio-thoracic surgeon and some say is far out of his expertise area when speaking about particular subjects; yet, thousands watch him every day and believe him to be an expert on all things related to health.

How do you become the expert?

First, quit worrying that you are NOT the expert or that you are a fraud. Instead, focus on what you can improve. Make sure the action steps you take to become an expert are steady and consistent. It may not happen overnight but before you know it, you will be considered an expert.

Continue to learn. An expert stays on top of the things in their field and in business. This does not necessarily mean going for additional training every other month. Instead, use Google reader to stay on top of news in your industry. You can even set up Google alerts so that when a new story comes out in your industry it will be emailed to you. Also, subscribe to and read your industry association publications.

To say the least we are bombarded with information every single minute of the day. This means being able to process and sort information quickly is essential. A great way to do this is to use a program called Photo Reading. This program allows you to subconsciously take pictures of pages and quickly comprehend and retain information with higher levels of accuracy. Setting yourself up as an expert might also mean writing articles, creating videos and speaking at events. We will talk more about this later in the book.

What are some action steps you can take?

Declare yourself an expert right here, right now.

Set up Google Alerts to come on a weekly basis.

Subscribe to industry association publications.

Investigate Photo Reading, which will save you lots of time.

Gail's Story – I started my own personal training business over 12 years ago. I quickly was known as the trainer who worked with individuals that were "at risk." How did I do it? I contacted every doctor in town to let them know this was my specialty. I even offered training sessions to the physicians and staff so they could see how I operated my business and that I safely trained individuals. I always updated the physicians on a quarterly basis by sending them a letter which they highly appreciated. In the end, I created long lasting relationships with these practices.

Additional Resources

www.google.com/reader
www.google.com/alerts
www.photoreading.com– Photo reading learning
program

BUSINESS MASTERY TIP #7

SIMPLE Websites & SEO Friendly Strategy

A website is an important part of your business. Less and less people check the yellow pages to see if you are a viable business; instead they check to see if you have a website. You do not have to get complex with your website - in fact often the simpler, the better.

The design of a website can be a very expensive venture. This is especially true if you do not know what you are looking for. So proceed with caution.

There are several basic website programs through which you can hire someone to set up the initial site or you can do it yourself. You will see some recommendations in the additional resource section.

So why have a website in the first place? Websites are designed for many reasons. Your website gives you credibility, helps you attract and retain clients, increase sales conversions and educate your visitors. Your website also helps build your "list". Your "list' is a term you will hear often. This is a list of names and email addresses of current paying clients and potential clients. The larger your list of ideal customers the easier it will be for you to build a profitable business.

Here are some things you must be aware of before doing anything.

You need to buy the domain and the hosting for the domain. DO NOT let a "web programming" company take care of this for you. If you do, they will have complete control of your site. If you own your site and host the domain and things do not work out with the web programming company, all you will have to do is change your username and password. If your web programmer buys the domain and hosts your site, you will be at their mercy if things do not work as you would like.

If you hire a website company:

Look at other people's websites and make notes of which websites appeal to you and why. Then contact them and ask who did their website setup and what program did they use. Most important, if they hired someone, were they satisfied?

Be sure the website company trains you to make basic website changes yourself so you do not have to call them for every minor issue. One thing you can do is take a non-credit course at the local college just to have some basic understanding of coding.

Get in writing exactly what the website company will do and the completion date for the website to go live. Have someone look at the contract who has knowledge of websites to make sure that everything is reasonable and fair.

DO NOT give any money up front. Unfortunately, there are too many disreputable companies that will take your deposit and disappear. Make sure the payment schedule is something you are comfortable with.

What are the "must have" basics?

Opt-in Box on your front page – you want to offer something of value for free. This is important to grow your list. Your clients and potential clients will complete a form with their email address and name to get your free offer. Opt-in boxes help you comply with anti-spam laws, which basically state that you can only send emails to people who request them from you. When someone double opts in, they are completing your web form and then clicking a link in a confirmation email that they get from your email provider confirming they wish to receive emails from you on a certain subject. You can easily create your opt-in form through your email marketing provider such as Aweber, Mail Chimp or Constant Contact. These services will also walk you through the process of creating the confirmation email that will automatically go out if you are using the double opt-in process.

About – be authentic and entertaining, not dry and boring. Let your website visitors have a peek at your personality.

Contact Us – if you have this page, make sure you answer all emails promptly.

Services – have one page with a list of all of your services and pictures and provide links to individual service pages that describe each service in more detail.

Products – set this up the same way as the services page. If you have a lot of products, you may want to use a shopping cart system.

Other pages you may want to add in the future are a Blog, Events and Partner pages.

Your sales pages for your products and services can be tricky business. You want to answer the following questions on every sale page that is created:

Why should someone buy your service or product?

How will it benefit the consumer?

What are the features?

How does it do what it does?

What creative things can the consumer-do with the product or service other than the obvious?

Are your sales pages easy to ready with larger font?

Do they include pictures and use captive headlines?

How do you make your website SEO friendly?

You have probably heard a lot about SEO optimization and keywords. These words can sound foreign and scary but they do not need to be. You can hire someone to do this for you or you can learn a few key basics that will help you with your website, articles, and videos that you create.

First, you need to understand what SEO means. Wikipedia defines it as: Search Engine Optimization (SEO) is the process of improving the visibility of a website or a web page in a search engine's "natural," or un-paid ("organic" or "algorithmic"), search results. In general, the earlier (or higher ranked on the search results page), and more frequently a site appears in the search results list, the more visitors it will receive from the search engine's users.

One way that people obtain a higher web page ranking is with keywords. Google adwords has a great free tool that you can use to determine if anyone is searching for a particular keyword or keyword phrase. You then use the results to determine the keywords for your website, articles and videos. Pick keywords that are low competition and preferably have 5,000-50,000 searches. Go for the lower hanging fruit. You will gravitate toward picking keywords that have millions of searches;

however, you will be able to move up the Google ranks quicker if you go for the smaller search numbers.

Because this can be confusing, we have created an easy, step-by-step video that you can watch to get a quick handle on exactly how to use keywords in your SEO strategy. See the Additional Resources section.

Choosing keywords that you can use regularly throughout your website will help you improve your SEO strategy. For instance, one of Holistic Marketing Mentors keyword phrases is "increase profits". We promise this to our customers in our website banner and throughout many of our blogs, products and other materials. It is one of our keywords and because it is appropriate to use in our content, it is easy to use as a keyword on multiple pages. You can easily see which keywords are used most often on your website with density checking tools. It is also helpful to know what keywords your industry leaders use most often on their website. See the Additional Resources section for a link to the SEO tools density checker.

Something else that will help improve your Google ranking is keeping your content fresh and unique. Do not just set up your website and forget it. Add new content and change your pages on a regular basis.

Back links should be another key element to your SEO strategy. Back links are also known as incoming links or inbound links to a website or web page. Build back links from other relevant and high-ranking sites.

Alexa provides an easy to understand free ranking of websites. The lower the number in Alexa, the higher the ranking in Google. The goal is to post your content on websites that rank better than yours which contain back links to pages on your website. Be creative and back link to different pages on your website. You can even utilize your keywords and create hyperlinks. If you do not understand this, do not concern yourself with it. Just do the best you can and come back to this another time.

One last thing to consider is the type of website you create. Certain website platforms will also affect your keyword ranking. Websites built with a WordPress platform tend to rank higher on Google quicker than some other platforms you can choose from.

What are some action steps you can take?

Decide if you are going to hire a website developer or do it yourself.

Whether you do it yourself or hire someone else, you will want to decide layouts for the following pages:

> About
> Contact Us
> Services
> Products
> Other pages

If you decide to do it yourself, find some good resources to walk you through setting up your basic website step-by-step. If you are building a WordPress website GFYD Member provides a lot of great tutorials and support to help even the beginner website newbie. See the Additional Resources section.

Create your website pages.

Decide what you will offer to build your list and make that your opt-in page.

Create your free offer and the auto responders to send to people as they sign up to receive it.

Do your keyword research.

Decide which keywords will be used on the front page of your website.

Decide which keywords will be used on most pages of your website.

Decide how often you will update and/or change your website's content.

Additional Resources

www.holisticmarketingmentors.com/mastery - Video on how to determine keywords

www.holisticmarketingmentors.com/mastery - Done for you website set up (WordPress, Dream Theme), website SEO optimization, optin form creation, email provider setup and auto responders

www.popupdomination.com – Easy pop-up optins

www.gfydmember.com – Step by step instructions on creating WordPress sites

www.mailchimp.com – Email marketing program

www.aweber.com – Email marketing program

www.constantcontact.com – Email marketing program

www.adwords.google.com – Keyword tool

www.seotools.seozy.com/tools/keyword-density-checker - Keyword density checker of your website and other websites

www.spyfu.com – Find out what other websites are using for keywords and adwords

SEO Made Simple (Second Edition): Strategies For Dominating The World's Largest Search Engine by Michael H. Fleischner

BUSINESS MASTERY TIP #8

SMART Systems and Testing Procedures

SMART Systems

The best advice in creating systems is to treat your business like a franchise. Everything that you do in your business should have a process. You never know when someone will want to collaborate with you or even buy your business and the worst thing that can happen is that you have to try to explain what you do and come across scattered and unorganized.

In addition, you will want systems in place as you hire employees so that it is easier to train them. You also need systems in place in case something happens to you or a loved one and your business needs to run without you for a short period of time.

How do you create systems?

This is certainly not going to be an overnight process, but in the end, it shows potential customers, employees, partners and buyers that you are serious about your business.

Think about this for a moment, what is your system when a customer calls? What do you say? How do you follow up? What do you send them? You get the idea. Someone should be able to step into your business tomorrow and be able to do what you do.

Make step-by-step lists of exactly what you do and how you do it. Keep all of your systems in an operations manual broken down by category in the computer. You may also want to keep a binder of your systems. Just make sure the computer and the hard copy version correlate at all times.

Remember that to be successful you need to not only work IN your business but you need to work ON your business.

What are some key actions steps you can take?

Schedule some time each week to work on your business.

Make a list of systems that you would like to put into place.

Decide which systems need to be created first.

Begin putting together your first system. When this is completed then start working on your next system.

SMART Testing Procedures

If you talk to any Internet marketing guru, they will tell you that there is no sense taking the time to market your business if you are not going to measure the effectiveness of it.

The best analogy is shooting darts at a dartboard blindfolded and hoping that you hit the board. You need to know what results you are getting so that you can tweak what is and is not working. Do not just give up and say social media doesn't work or blogging doesn't work. It does work; you just have to perfect your strategy.

Entrepreneurs never give up; they persevere, and they are tenacious. Think of Colonel Sanders at KFC. He was rejected over 30 times with his recipe. Henry Ford failed and went broke five times before he succeeded. Thomas Edison failed his first 1,000 attempts at making the light bulb. However, when asked, "How did it feel to fail 1,000 times?" Edison replied, "I didn't fail 1,000 times. The light bulb was an invention with 1,000 steps."

Don't get discouraged; just keep looking at how it can be better.

Keep this strategy in mind with your marketing.

How do you set up testing procedures?

This is a matter of testing. No seriously, you will find some things work better than others. We talk more about the best practices and how to set up many of the things you will be testing later in this book. However, for this section you need to know that the main areas you want to test are your email open and click through rates; your website statistics; your social media reach and engagement rates; and the effectiveness of your articles.

The simplest thing you can measure is whether your customers are opening your emails and the links in your emails. This can be done through your email marketing service such as Mailchimp, Aweber or Constant Contact. If you are getting a low open rate, try changing the title or the format of your emails.

On your website, you can track how many people visit each page and how long they are staying on a page. Google has an easy program called Google Analytics that you can install and embed code onto your website to look at these statistics.

In the Additional Resources section you will see a link to a sample spreadsheet you can use to track your important key statistics. You will also see a spreadsheet you can use to test different marketing strategies.

You will also want to track the results of your social media efforts. You can look at how many people are re-tweeting your twitter posts and liking or commenting in Facebook and Google+.

To measure your influence on Twitter try using Klout. Klout measures over 30 factors and gives you a ranking from 1 to 100. Check out your Klout ranking and others in your industry. Retweet Rank is another tool that you can use to find out how many times your twitter account has been retweeted and your ranking based on this calculation.

Facebook has a nice analytic tool called Insights that does exactly what the word sounds like. It gives you insight as to how well your Facebook posts are engaging your audience, how many likes you have, where they are coming from and what your audience demographics are. See the Additional Resources section for a step-by-step tutorial on how to use Facebook Insights.

You can see how effective Google+ is for your business in your Google Analytics.

Another thing you will want to measure is how well your opt-in is converting. Your opt-in is the freebie or special you are advertising on your front page of your website and through other marketing efforts to create a larger list. Your email-marketing program will give you specific statistics on how well your opt-in is performing. Change it out regularly to test different things like colors, wording, pictures and special offers.

You will also want to measure the effectiveness of your articles. Make sure each article links back to a page on your site. If the site you are posting your article on won't allow this then have a link in your bio. You will want to know if there are certain types of articles or subjects that do better than others. Find out which article marketing sites generate more referral traffic to your website. Also, pay attention to who is commenting on your articles. Make sure you respond back quickly.

If you would like to see some basic statistics of other websites from leaders and peers in your industries you can install SEO Quake. This will tell you their page rank for Google, Yahoo and Bing, number of backlinks, etc. This is a nifty little tool; have fun seeing how you measure up.

What are some key actions steps you can take?

If you do not have an email-marketing program, get one.

Install Google Analytics on your website.

Install SEO Quake on your computer.

Install the Alexa tool bar.

Download the free templates for testing email, website, social media and article marketing.

Additional Resources

www.mailchimp.com – Email marketing program
www.aweber.com – Email marketing program
www.constantcontact.com – Email marketing program
www.analytics.google.com – Google analytics website statistics
www.seoquake.com - Statistics of other people's websites
www.alexa.com – Check Alexa rankings
www.holisticmarketingmentors.com/mastery - Templates for testing email, website, social media and article marketing
www.klout.com – Measures your Twitter influence
www.retweetrank.com – Measures how your tweets rank

CLIENT MASTERY

Customers make or break your business. Without them, a business does not exist. However, many of us take our customers for granted, especially after they become part of our database. If you treat your customers like family, you will have long-standing clients and you will have them referring people to you month after month, year after year.

Did you know that it takes ten times the amount of time, money and energy to get a new client as it does to keep your current clients? So why do we neglect our customers even though they are important to us?

Think about your own business. Is your current list of customers at the top of your priority list? Or have you become complacent thinking that they will continue returning to you for their needs?

Even if you are good about telling and showing your clients how much they mean to you, there is always room for improvement. It does not matter if your clients are active or inactive. It is imperative to your success that you make "touches" with them on a consistent basis.

So what are some keys to client mastery? You will be surprised at some of these tips.

CLIENT MASTERY TIP #1

CLIENT Personality Types

We have all heard of personality types and often when we hear this, we think of the Meyers Brigg testing. The Meyers Brigg testing is wonderful and very in depth. However, it can be confusing and difficult to implement instantaneously. The evaluation is long and intensive and probably the last thing you want to ask your "new" client to do.

But, it is important to determine your clients personality immediately so that you can create a stronger, long-term relationship without a lot of frustration. Understanding personality types also allows you to have a better understanding of your own strengths and weaknesses so that you are better able to deal with other personalities.

How do you determine personality types?

Determining personality types quickly and accurately is actually quite easy. All you need to know are a few key characteristics plus what motivates each personality type and you are on your way. Once you know these things, you will know how to interact with your client, what their strengths and weaknesses are likely to be and how they like to be approached and appreciated.

In order to retain happier, loyal clients show them that you truly understand who they are and what is important to them.

For the purposes of this book, the personality types are divided into four groups. Some of the traits and characteristics have been developed with the assistance of one of our mentors, Jennifer Hough.

Keep in mind that most people are a combination of personality types. However, you will find one personality type is usually more dominant in each individual.

Personality Type: Owls

How are Owls motivated?

> Owls are motivated by numbers and facts.

Key Characteristics

> Analytical, love instructions, often take perfect notes, orderly, rules were meant to be followed, very detailed and organized, on time, perfectionists, do their own bookkeeping, diligent, hardworking, not easily intimidated. Owls often ask the difficult questions, speak as though they are interrogating someone and ask questions that begin with "why". They are very practical and predictable and they can see the upside and downside to a problem. Owls often wait to talk because they are thinking.

How well do Owls communicate?

>Owls are good listeners but are often thought of as weak communicators because they do not have good people skills. Owls are also sometimes thought of as being insensitive and cold hearted. Be careful because Owls do not like to be interrupted when they are talking.

How do Owls show empathy?

>Owls often mistake other people's moods and feelings to be about them. They need to work harder at being empathetic towards others and realize that someone's bad mood, anxiety or depression has nothing to do with them.

Clothing

>Owls tend to wear dark and dated clothing. Men usually wear collared shirts. They are a little more straight laced with their clothing choices.

Music

>Owls typically enjoy classical or heavy metal music.

Car

>Owls like to drive something practical and well-researched. Their vehicles get good gas mileage and hold up well if in an accident.

Strengths

Owls are known for their wisdom and discernment. They are very credible.

Weaknesses

Owls take forever to make decisions; they ask for a lot of information and can be high maintenance.

Ways to appreciate Owls

Appreciate your Owl clients when they comply with the protocol you give them. Honor them and their values. Appreciate their organization skills and their attention to details.

Interacting with Owls

Be professional and respectful. Do not be loud, outgoing or invade their space. Do not touch your Owl client except for the handshake. Be honest and make eye contact. Listen well, do not interrupt them, and do not be aggressive.

Words to use when speaking to Owls

Unacceptable, checked, typically, affirmative, issues, mistake, loyalty, qualified, top position, effective, efficient, error, inconvenient, issue, appropriate, inappropriate, and timely. Give full titles upon introduction and do not use abbreviations or slang.

When marketing to an Owl

> Owls are about processes and operations. They need to know "how" something works.

When your client is an Owl

> If they are asking questions that is a good thing. Make sure you are thorough with your answers. Do not be vague. Ask "Do you have enough information to make a decision?" If no, then ask, "What else do you need?" Do not rush them. Follow up with additional reading materials including research studies. They like newsletters with detailed information.

If you are an Owl

> You are great at maintaining control of situations – realize though that not everyone is perfect and will not follow your protocols perfectly. Be forgiving and encouraging to clients to continue to try their best. Do not assume everyone likes details. Be attentive but be careful not to interrogate.

Personality Type: Dolphins

How are Dolphins motivated?

> Dolphins are motivated by fun.

Key Characteristics

Life of the party, optimistic, enthusiastic, high energy, spontaneous, enjoys change, likes groups, loves to be the center of attention, does not like silence, and soaks up everything, creative and good in team settings. Dolphins are also often late and believe that rules were meant to be broken. Their cars are a mess and they lack organization skills. Dolphins are natural promoters of what they believe in. They want to be appreciated and recognized. Dolphins are also likely to only give you their first name when introducing themselves.

How well do Dolphins communicate?

Dolphins are infectious and people like to be around them. They talk a lot but do not listen well.

How do Dolphins show empathy?

Dolphins, like Owls mistake other people's moods and feelings to be about them. They need to work harder at being empathetic towards others and realize that someone's bad mood, anxiety or depression has nothing to do with them.

Clothing

Dolphins typically are "hip", dress in bright colors and love accessories.

Music

Dolphins love a variety of music.

Car

Dolphins drive fun cars that fit their personality and higher end vehicles. They also like personalized license plates.

Strengths

People like to do what Dolphins do and be around them. They motivate and encourage others easily. Dolphins are great sales people.

Weaknesses

Dolphins have difficulties staying focused, are unorganized and change their minds often. Dolphins need to listen more.

Ways to appreciate Dolphins

Dolphins like souvenirs from trips, public recognition, and high fives.

Interacting with Dolphins

You will want to have a strong handshake and smile. Have lots of energy. Do not be timid, boring or stiff. Do not give first and last name on introduction.

Words to use when speaking to Dolphins

Everyone loves, coolest, fun, and amazing.

When marketing to a Dolphin

These people have no patience. They need to know why. Do not give them the details - give them the benefits. What is it going to do for them?

When your client is a Dolphin

Dolphins have to trust you. They want to know that you care about what is important to them. Watch them closely, email them, and give them audios. Show them you care. Call them and send them personal emails checking in with them. Give them compliments. They like newsletters that give them information they are interested in and that are personalized.

If you are a Dolphin

Get a bookkeeper and someone to keep you organized. You need to have good assistants to maintain control and focus. Remember to be quiet more often and to listen to others.

Personality Type: Tigers

How are Tigers motivated?

Tigers are motivated by the challenge.

Key Characteristics

> Like to lead and can have difficulty following, want to be perceived as the best, to the point and do not do small talk well. They are determined, goal oriented, rarely give up, do not like to take "no" for an answer, get things done quickly, are multi-taskers, live on adrenalin, and are very intense and productive. They are quick decision makers, very daring, strong-willed, rebellious, do not care about fitting in, are direct, do not mind making wrong decisions, and they like to give instructions. Tigers are blind to their weaknesses, have lots of confidence and are risk takers.

How well do Tigers communicate?

> Tigers are good communicators and tend to be excellent writers. However, they need to slow down and stop multi-tasking in order to listen well.

How do Tigers show empathy?

> Tigers understand how others are feeling, and are genuinely concerned with others. Their natural empathy and caring is effective at helping others through problems. Even though Tigers may understand how others feel, they are often so focused that they bulldoze

through people. They need to slow down in order not to do this.

Clothing

Tigers typically dress well; women like heels.

Music

Tigers like Rock 'n' Roll.

Car

Tigers like things that are fast. If they do not drive a convertible, it is likely to be a vehicle that they can put a lot of stuff in.

Strengths

Tigers get a lot done and make quick decisions. Tend to excel in many things.

Weaknesses

Tigers say yes to everything. Can be abrupt, do not slow down and listen well, cut people off a lot. They intimidate Golden Retrievers. Tigers have a hard time being teachable, get defensive easily and are poor time managers.

Ways to appreciate

Tigers like to have their achievements and values appreciated. They like feeling like they are getting the best, including expensive gifts and name brands.

Interacting with Tigers

Tigers prefer direct interaction, to the point and respectful of their time. Do not be fearful or timid of this personality.

Words to use when speaking to Tigers

Innovative, creative, error, busy, fast, quickest, value your time, awesome, value, you are important, apologize for any inconvenience.

When marketing to a Tiger

Tigers are advocates and creators. In order to keep them from quickly dismissing your offer, you need to quickly show them the opportunity. Tell them how can they can benefit or use your product for something beyond the obvious.

When your client is a Tiger

They do not have the time to read emails or other materials. If they love you, they will recommend you to all of their friends and acquaintances. Get them to take their power back and to slow down enough to take care of themselves. They like follow up but be quick and to the point. Do not waste their time with lots of useless information. Leaving messages are great; do not expect them to call you back.

If you are a Tiger

You are good at keeping control of situations and remaining on task. You need to be careful of not giving clients too much information or changes to do at once. Do not be hectic or frantic. Slow down and listen to clients. It is okay to stay on time but do not act as if you are rushing clients. Work hard at making people feel more comfortable.

Personality Type: Golden Retrievers

How are Golden Retrievers motivated?

Golden Retrievers are motivated by helping others even if they have to sacrifice something.

Key Characteristics

Love people, like to feel needed, relaxed and peaceful in nature, want to blend in, hate confrontation and do not like to rock the boat. They are easy to be with, introverted, naturally compliant, can be indecisive, "clutter bugs", are sentimental, arrive early, leave late, do not care about being number one and are for a cause.

How well do Golden Retrievers communicate?

Golden Retrievers are great listeners and soft-spoken.

How do Golden Retrievers show empathy?

> Golden Retrievers understand how others are feeling, and are genuinely concerned with others. Their natural empathy and caring is effective at helping others through problems. They need to be careful not to be so empathetic that they take on their clients issues. Golden Retrievers need to remember that their role is to help the client feel better even if they need to convince the client to do things to help themselves that they may not want to do.

Clothing

> Clothes are loose and comfortable and non-restrictive.

Music

> Golden Retrievers like soothing music.

Car

> Golden Retrievers prefer something that will accommodate the most people such as a minivan.

Strengths

> Golden Retrievers love being of service to the world.

Weaknesses

> Golden Retrievers are easy to manipulate because they feel guilty for making a profit and they do not ask for what they need.

Ways to appreciate

> Golden Retrievers like sentimental gifts, notes appreciating their general interests. For example, a note with a sunset that is peaceful.

Interacting with Golden Retrievers

> Golden Retrievers prefer someone who is soft spoken and personal. They like to be touched. They shy away from those that are loud and outgoing.

Words to use when speaking to Golden Retrievers

> Personal, family, visiting, hands on, support, blessing, heart and help.

When marketing to a Golden Retriever

> Golden Retrievers want to know what the objective of the service is and/or product and what are the outcomes. They need you to answer the "what for" and give them the expected results.

When your client is a Golden Retriever

> Golden Retrievers want you to care about them and humanity. They do not like aggressiveness. Plan to spend more time listening to them. Following up with the Golden Retriever is very important. This can be done by phone, email or card. Just be concerned with touching base with them and seeing how they are doing. Acknowledge something that is important to them.

If you are a Golden Retriever

> Use your strong listening skills but speak up and take charge. You need to be assertive to end appointments on time and to make appropriate recommendations. You need to tell your clients what they need to do. Working from scripts can help even though they will feel uncomfortable to begin with.

All personality types love having you use their name. It has been said that the best sound in the human language is hearing someone say your name.

What are key actions steps you can take?

Study one personality type each week.

Practice determining personality types. What are your friends and families personality types?

Note your clients' personality type with their client information.

Follow up with your clients using their personality type.

Additional Resources

www.holisticmarketingmentors.com/mastery - Printable personality types with personality grid

CLIENT MASTERY TIP #2

LOVING your Clients

It sounds so ridiculous, but customer service is at an all-time low. Take notice the next time you are out and about. People are just miserable. So why not stand out above the crowd?

Customer appreciation is a great way to let your customers know you love them and value their business. It can be an annual party, monthly or quarterly giveaways, or newsletters giving useful information. Show your clients that you truly care about them.

How do you show your clients that you love them?

One great example is a Philadelphia personal trainer's way of taking care of her customers.

> *Terry's Story - Terry has a large personal training business in a town of approximately 500,000 people. Every year on the first Saturday of December from 6-10 pm, she has a drop in holiday party at the same place. She has great food, drinks and prizes. She invites every client of hers over the past 15 years. Kids are welcome too. Last year she had just over 3,000 people drop in during the four hour time period. She takes time to talk to each and every person that walks through her door.*

Well, you might be saying this is too expensive. You are right it is not cheap. However, she has never spent any money on traditional advertising. It is just a matter of where you want to spend your advertising dollars.

Think of something on a smaller scale that you can do. Customers that feel like they are heard and appreciated will keep coming back and will be your best source of advertising.

Contests are another great way to appreciate clients and even attract new ones. You can utilize contests to get customers and potential customers to Like your Facebook fan page, share posts or even register for a list. Use contests to appreciate your current clientele. A great example would be a "refer a friend" program. Every time someone refers a friend, they get a chance to win a trip, TV, etc. The more people they refer, the better their chances of winning. Contests are a great way to create enthusiasm and anticipation in a group.

Remember your number one goal with your client is to make them "feel" good and to soothe them. They come to you because they have a problem and need your help solving it. Begin to help them immediately by soothing them and making them feel important. Show your clients you appreciate and love them for who they are. Be in the present moment with them.

What are some key actions steps you can take?

Make a list of different ways you can appreciate your customers.

Prioritize this list and begin with the first few ways.

Schedule client appreciation days and times on your calendar.

Create a contest to appreciate existing clients.

Create a contest to attract new clients.

Additional Resources

www.sendoutcards.com – Easy and inexpensive way to send out thank you, birthday, anniversary and congratulation cards quickly.
www.shop4freebies.com – Free gift ideas
www.overstock.com – Inexpensive gift ideas

CLIENT MASTERY TIP #3

IDEAL Customers

It is important to narrow your customer base down to a smaller manageable size. To say that everyone is your customer is wasting your time and your money. Do you have millions of dollars to market to such a large customer base? Do you have tons of employees to do this effectively?

If you answered "no" to these questions, then you need to narrow this down. The more you narrow it down the more effective your marketing will be and the quicker you will become known as the expert in your niche.

For example, if you are a nutritionist, how will people be able to differentiate you from your peers? You may have dozens or hundreds of other nutritionists in your immediate area. When someone asks for a referral from someone on Facebook for a nutritionist to help a family member with diabetes how will they know to refer them to you? They will not. They will think of the half a dozen nutritionists they know and it will be a matter of chance that you are the one they refer. However, if everyone knows that you are the Diabetes expert on nutrition than you will be the only one they think of even if they have never met you. Do not leave your business to chance instead niche it down.

Narrowing down your niche is imperative to getting exposure. You might have heard the saying, "Narrowing down your niche, makes you rich." This is certainly a key component in your success.

The more specific you are, the easier it is to gain access to your ideal clients and to tell others what you are looking for. You might ask but isn't this narrowing down my focus too much? What if someone comes up to me and wants to do business with me but it does not fit into my niche? Of course, you can work with them. You do not need to turn them away. However, be aware your ideal client is someone you are passionate about. If you work with someone you do not really care for than this leaves less time to devote to the clients that bring you the most joy.

You have to ask yourself that even if this person does not fit your ideal client profile; do you still want to work with them? Answer from your heart and not from scarcity. Do not take on clients solely because you need the money. This will spell disaster.

Not niching down is one of the biggest mistakes we see wellness professionals making. You may not want to niche down because you are afraid you will leave money on the table. You may decide you cannot niche down because you cannot make up your mind what you want to focus on.

Let us be very clear on this subject. If you do not niche down, you are definitely leaving money on the table. If you do not niche down you will not have the laser focus needed to make your business successful the way you want.

How do you go about narrowing down your ideal client or niche?

Ask yourself some questions:

What does my ideal client look like?

What sex are they?

What age group?

What demographics – income, marital status, etc.?

Where do they work, go to school, and hang out?

What are they wearing?

What are they afraid of?

What do they do for fun?

What are their biggest challenges?

What do they go to sleep worrying about?

What pain are you solving for them? Is there a market for this?

What other problems do they have?

Who do they see for these other problems?

What makes them happy?
Where do they spend their money?

What are some key actions steps you can take?

Determine your ideal client/niche by answering the questions above.

Start talking to them and find out if they really need your services or products.

Ask them if they would purchase your services and/or products.

Develop a marketing plan that targets your ideal clients.

Write articles, give video tips, distribute newsletters that help your ideal clients with their problems, as you have identified.

Additional Resources

www.holisticmarketingmentors.com/mastery - Who is your ideal client questionnaire

CLIENT MASTERY TIP #4

EVALUATING Clients

Oh, success at last, you have the client in your office, now what? First, you need to evaluate them. Sounds like a simple process yet many take this step for granted and gloss over it. Instead, take time with it. This is where the client truly begins to connect with you not only a clinical level but also on a personal level.

How should you prepare?

First – Create client intake forms. Have your client complete any forms prior to meeting with you. Organize the completed forms neatly in a folder.

Second – Review all forms thoroughly before meeting with the client. Make a list of additional questions for them.

Third – Shut up and listen. Yes, we know you have an agenda, but the client came to you because they need to be heard and understood. Find out what is really pulling at their heartstrings. What are they seeking? What are their pains? Encourage and soothe them.

Fourth – Determine their personality type and do not hesitate to review their personality type with them to be sure you have assessed them correctly.

Fifth – Wait through "the pause." It is ok to be silent. Most people hate silence and will begin to talk again. Give them the floor.

Sixth – Ask opened ended questions that you have prepared ahead of time. Again, they want to be heard and this gives them a chance to tell their "story."

Seventh – Lay the ground rules. Tell them exactly what you expect of them and what they can expect from you and how you can help them.

Eighth – Be sure to ask them if they have any additional questions or concerns.

Nine – Set their next appointment. Preferably, payments should be collected prior to the consult. If you collect payment at the end be sure not to get side tracked and forget to collect their money.

Ten – Always have clients complete a "rating checklist" at their next (follow up) appointment/consult. This allows the client to tell you their current issues/problems. This checklist provides a guide for them and you since many will forget what problems are at the top of their list. This will also show the improvement that the client is seeing over time and the areas that still need to be addressed.

You can have your clients rate each item on a scale of 1 to 10. Each time they have an appointment/consult, the client can then see for themselves the progress they are making and the reasons to continue following your protocol.

This checklist works for any profession to show progress and puts the control and the expectations back in the client's hands.

What are some key actions steps you can take?

Create the forms necessary for a complete evaluation.

Have a system to evaluate each client/patient and do not stray from it.

Be very clear with each client on what it will take to see results. Tell them what they can expect from you and vice versa.

Create a ratings checklist.

Additional Resources

www.holisticmarketingmentors.com/mastery -
Sample patient form
www.holisticmarketingmentors.com/mastery -
Sample ratings checklist

CLIENT MASTERY TIP #5

NOTEWORTHY Follow Ups

A good follow up system is imperative if you strive for excellent customer service. Do you struggle with following up with your clients? Is it because you are afraid of being too pushy? If this is the case, how often do you really get upset when someone follows up with you? You probably do not get upset when people follow up very often, if at all; in fact follow up is so rare in today's world that if you do this important step you will stand head and shoulders above your peers.

Try putting yourself in your client's shoes. Would you want a follow up email or phone call? We live in such a fast-paced society that taking this extra step may sometimes seem like it is just too much trouble. You might think that no one really appreciates it. Nevertheless, your clients do like knowing you care, even if they do not say anything. Remember, successful people are the ones that go the extra mile and are the professionals who win in the long run. We bet your clients are worth going the extra mile.

How do you follow up with excellence?

24 hours after their appointment send them an email or give them a call. Thank them for their

business and ask if they have any questions. Be sure to smile while you are on the phone with them (it will change your energy) and if you get them "live" on the phone, always ask if they have a minute to spare; never assume that they have time to talk with you. You want them to be happy when they get off the phone with you and it is important that they know you value their time.

48 hours after their appointment send your client some information. Be sure you understand their personality type since some individuals hate long emails and even research studies; some people love them. Be sure to appeal to their personality.

Send them a friendly reminder of their next appointment which should have been scheduled in the prior consult.

Something else you can do is to provide your current clients and potential clients with valuable information on a regular basis. Provide them with an e-zine or newsletter that includes tips on how to stay healthy, healthy recipes, tips, etc. You could also include something on local events that might interest them.

Consistency is important. Continue to be in contact with your clients on a regular basis, even if they are no longer seeing you for your services or making purchases.

If you cannot make the phone calls or touch base regularly, have a virtual assistant do it for you. If you think you do not even have time to write a newsletter, have Holistic Marketing Mentors do it for you. All of the content is provided, so all you need to do is plug and send.

One of the quickest ways to rise to the top of your industry is to develop excellent follow up skills. Do this and not only will the people you come into contact with love you but you will also find more joy in serving them.

What are some key actions steps you can take?

Call or email after appointments.

Email tips and other useful information on a regular basis.

Send cards or call on their birthday, anniversary, and other milestones.

Give them small tokens of appreciation.
Hire a virtual assistant or a newsletter service, if needed.

Be of service and go over and above their expectations. Help them out with things like pet sitting, making food when they are not feeling well.

Traci's Story – There have been so many times in my life where following up with my clients and going that extra mile have helped me be more successful than others who were just as qualified. What I discovered is when your clients and employees know who you are and "feel" that you really care about what matters to them, they will give back way beyond your expectations. This was very apparent when my husband and I owned a small group fitness center called Cardio Fit.

When we started Cardio Fit we were not thinking of owning a gym. We just wanted a place where we could spin. It started one morning when our local gym announced they were closing their doors. We were devastated. We had started spinning classes several months earlier and we were addicted. We finally had a workout that we enjoyed verses always dreading the days we had to exercise.

We talked with a few people and our instructor and we decided to buy some spin bikes and start a small spin class with our local Parks and Recreation Department. Before we knew it we had other instructors coming to us wanting to teach aerobics, kickboxing, Pilates, yoga and more. Members followed us and we started attracting even more people.

Our whole premise for starting Cardio Fit was that it was community; we were one big family. We communicated with our instructors regularly, by email and having group lunches. We asked for their advice and what they wanted and needed from us to make it a more enjoyable experience for them. We listened and implemented their suggestions. We also did this with our members. We found out what they wanted, we recognized their birthdays and accomplishments. We sent out a monthly newsletter keeping everyone updated with what was going on and giving people kudos for helping out around the gym, coming up with great ideas and reaching personal fitness goals.

We were family. Because of this, our instructors helped me tremendously when my husband had to work out of town because the downturn in the housing market had made it difficult for him to make money as a builder. We eventually sold Cardio Fit. However, years later my instructors still reach out and tell me how much they appreciated my communication skills. I still hear from members and they tell me how much they miss us. At Cardio Fit they felt like they were important and people truly cared about them.

Following up is not a marketing tactic. It shows you truly care.

Additional Resources

www.holisticmarketingmentors.com/mastery - Plug and send newsletter service

www.mailchimp.com – Free email service provider

www.aweber.com – Email service provider

www.vworker.com - Virtual assistants

www.asksunday.com - Virtual assistants

www.b2kcorp.com - Virtual assistants

www.taskseveryday.com – Virtual assistants; must hire 20 to 40 hours per week

CLIENT MASTERY TIP #6

TAKING Care of Objections

Hearing a client tell you NO is always difficult. You need to understand that you are not trying your hardest unless you are getting lots of no's on a daily basis. Objections are great because they offer clarity to the interested party. Your goal is to have your schedule full of recurring clients. You cannot get here if you are too scared to hear the word "no".

It often takes many "no's" before you get a "yes". Rejections are a fact of life. Do not get discouraged. You are not being rejected personally. Your services and products are not meant for every person on this planet. These "no's" eliminate the individuals who are not a fit for you or your business.

A great way to think of this is by saying, "next" in your mind just as if they were the next person in line at the movie theater. There is always someone else around the corner.

Jack Canfield's _Chicken Soup for the Soul_ book was rejected by 123 publishers before he got his first "yes". Jack learned something called The Rule of Fives. If you go to a tree with a sharp axe every day and take five swings with the axe, eventually the tree, however big, will fall down. Jack Canfield decided to do five things each and every day to promote his book, even if he was rejected all five times.

The best way to handle objections is to be prepared. Go back and review the personality types. This is a great way to understand what types of objections may arise depending on your potential client's personality type and how you can more favorably respond to them. This will help you create ease and flow in the conversation and get more new clients to do business with you.

The definition of insanity is doing the same thing repeatedly and expecting different results. Do not drive yourself insane with objections. Learn how to handle them more effectively. When you review your day, do not focus on the "no's" you received. Instead, focus on your successes. Where you put your attention is what you will receive more of.

How to respond to objections?

Try responding to objections by their personality types.

Owls with numbers and facts.

Dolphins with what it will do for them; how will they feel.

Tigers with results, testimonials or stories; how can they use the product or service in a way that they may not have thought of.

Golden Retrievers with if they feel better themselves they will be able to help more people.

Refer back to the chapter discussing personality types for additional information or print the personality grid using the link in our Additional Resources section.

The following is one of the most common objections you will receive and suggestions on how to answer it.

Objection: I don't have the money.

General Tips and Response: This could be a stall or they truly may not have the money. Find out by asking them to explain it a little further. You could say, Tell me more about that. If you intuitively feel they have a money issue, perhaps offer a discounted rate for x visits or for the first months products. If not, explain, It is a matter of priorities. You can never replace your health and once you lose it, it is much harder to regain it. OR Looking good makes you feel better in every area of your life. It is priceless and you cannot put a price tag on this.

Responding to the Owl: I understand that you may not have budgeted for this service/product at this time and it is important to give it the appropriate consideration so that there are no mistakes in your treatment plan. However, unless you have some questions that still need to be answered, I do think that this is the best plan of action and it will save you x amount of dollars over the long run, are you sure that we can't move forward today?

Responding to the Dolphin: I know that this is something you were not planning for. However, if you were able to find the money now you would be able to receive x and y benefits in z amount of time. This will help you feel x. Our happy clients also love our referral program because they are able to earn x dollars toward future visits when clients they refer to us complete their first exam, training session, therapeutic session, etc. I am sure that you will see the results you are looking for if you follow the instructions I have given you and by giving us referrals you will also be saving you money.

Responding to the Tiger: I hear you and I don't want you to put yourself in a financial bind. However, if you were able to find the money to do this, you could see x and y results in as little as z weeks. This will give you the additional energy and mental clarity you need to be at the top of your game and I know that is important to you. I feel confident that you will see the results we have discussed because of the successful outcomes we have had with other clients.

Responding to the Golden Retriever: I understand. When do you feel you will have the money for x? Okay, is there any way you can find a way to pay for it sooner? The reason why I ask is because I know how important taking care of x and y are to you and so often I see my clients putting themselves last. I just want you to be able to feel your best so that you can take care of the things and people that are important to you. If you are not feeling well, I know you can't be of service the way you want to.

What are some key actions steps you can take?

The more practice, the better you will be; role-play with others to improve.

Follow Jack Canfield's advice – do five things each day to build your business.

Keep track of your clients' objections.

Determine how you can handle your most frequent objections. What can you say in response that might get a different result?

Look at overcoming your common objections earlier in the process before they bring them up.

Think of "next" in your head; there are plenty of other fish in the sea.

Additional Resources

Secrets of Closing the Sale by Zig Ziglar
Selling Your Services: Proven Strategies for Getting Clients to Hire You by Robert Bly
www.youtube.com/watch?v=4iCd2BqoFkk - Video on Fear of Rejection by Jack Canfield

MARKETING MASTERY

Marketing your business is vital to its success. You might have heard if a person is great at marketing, they can sell anything.

You might have experienced this in your own personal life where you bought something and when you got it home, you wondered how did that happen? You did not plan on buying the item, but something happened when you were in the store. It is as if a spell was cast over you and you were no longer in control of your thoughts or your wallet.

Great marketers listen for the customer's pain points and offer solutions to alleviate the pain. This is just the tip of the marketing iceberg. We used some of the same techniques in the last chapter when we discussed handling objections. This next section of the book will give you greater details on several suggestions that will take you to the top of your marketing game.

MARKETING MASTERY TIP #1

MAGNIFICENT Videos

If you want to get your message out to the world, it is imperative to get it out there in a big way. We are bombarded with messages these days and with all of the techie gadgets and social media sites we are inundated with companies trying to get us to spend our hard earned money.

In order for people to take you seriously, they must consider you an expert in your field and the easiest way to do this is to get exposure in various ways. This includes making short informative videos, blogging and article marketing which are all discussed in this section of the book.

Just like everything else, taking on too much at once will spell disaster and in a matter of days or weeks quitting and not doing it at all will be at the forefront of your mind. Pick something that resonates with you. If you have a desire to make videos start there. If you like writing focus on blogs or article writing and skip the next few pages.

Where do you get the content for your videos?

You actually have a wide variety of easy content at your fingertips. Keep a notebook to write down ideas that come to you. You can also convert any articles that you have written to multiple videos. Remember, you want to keep your videos short and to the point. Here are some video topic ideas:
Answer frequently asked questions.

Give tips to your clients that will help them follow protocols easier.

Give general health and wellness tips.

Make "How to" videos on a particular topic.

You will want to have a clear purpose for each video you create and not just post your content. What do you want the viewer to do next? Then create an easy way for them to do the next step.

So what are some possible next steps?

They could opt-in to your list. You could give two tips on your video and then have them complete an opt-in form to get tips 3 through 10 or even a free e-book or purchase a long end product.

You might use a video to generate more likes/followers on your social media sites or bring viewers to a specific page on your website. The possibilities are endless.

How do you effectively create your videos?

Your videos do not need to be complicated or long, but they do need to be informative, short and to the point. Attention spans are getting shorter and shorter. In fact, the latest statistics show videos less than one minute are viewed at a much higher rate. Professionals and celebrities may be able to go three to seven minutes without losing the viewer's attention span.

You will not need any complicated video equipment. In fact, when surveyed, individuals who watch videos say they prefer homemade videos instead of those made professionally. They feel they are more authentic.

You can get a HD video camera for less than $100 and you will also want to get a lavaliere microphone. This really improves the sounds quality. Backdrops can be anything from a blank wall; a decorated bookcase or wall; or even outside in your yard or at the local park. A video stand and a remote control are not bad ideas either. All of this is less than a $200 investment.

One word of caution is to be sure your video camera is compatible with your editing software. For example, the Kodak ZI8 is published in a .mov file and the Sony Vegas software only edits in an .mp4 format.

If you need to convert a file to another format, a great tool is Hamster Video Converter. It is free and will convert videos into a variety of formats. However, this is just another step in the process and if you can avoid it by creating your video in the format that you will need for editing and uploading you will appreciate the time you save.

Always have several video ideas ready to tape in one day so that you can record them all at once. Last, as you get more comfortable with the process you will want to talk into the camera off the top of your head and not read anything. If you want to have something scripted, there are free teleprompters you can use on your computer which scroll the text at the speed you select.

What are some action steps you can take?

Purchase camera and accessories that best suit your needs. Talk to some colleagues and ask what they use.

Brainstorm ideas for video topics.

Decide format for your videos – intro, exit, music, call to action, etc.

Create your music and graphic files or hire someone to create them.

How do you market your video?

In order to maximize your exposure you will want to submit your videos to multiple locations.

Begin with loading your videos to You Tube. Eventually you can load them to other video sites.

Once you have created your You Tube account you can easily load your videos. To optimize your videos with a SEO (search engine optimization) strategy there are a few key things that you will need to do to ensure that your videos get seen by more people.

First

Title your video with keywords that you have targeted for your website. Make sure your title is interesting and catches the eye of the audience. Some great titles are "How to", "X Tips", etc. You can also use a headline analyzer to determine the emotional value of your title. Look in the Additional Resource section for more details.

Second

If you have editing capabilities, like Camtasia, Sony Vegas or Jing video editor, add your website name to the bottom of your video. You may want to add a short introduction and conclusion to the video. However, this is not mandatory. Just get out there and do something.

Third

The first thing in your description should be a link to a page on your website, followed by a description of what is in the video using targeted keywords. Be sure the description makes sense and is not just a bunch of keyword phrases.

Fourth

Mark your video as "public". Then pick a screen shot where you look presentable and your mouth is not hanging open in an unflattering manner. If you are not careful this will be the first impression you make to potential clients and it is not so pretty.

Fifth

Take time to categorize your video. In many cases, it will fall under "how to."

Sixth

In the keyword or tag section, use keywords that are relevant to your business and to the video. Remember, Google Adwords is a great place research keywords.

Seventh

Load the video to You Tube then post it on your website. Once you are confident with posting to You Tube, try posting your video to at least two of the sites below in the Additional Resources section. Consistency is more important than volume so if it is too overwhelming than just post your videos on You Tube only. Do not forget, you can always outsource this step for a relatively small amount of money.

Eighth

Post your videos on social media sites such as:
Facebook
Twitter
LinkedIn
Google Plus

Ninth

Post to bookmarking sites to attract additional viewers, such as:
Stumbleupon
Digg
Delicious
Google Buzz
Technorati

What are some key actions steps you can take?

Decide if you are going to write articles or produce videos first and become proficient at it.

If you choose videos, continue on here, if you choose articles go to the next section.

Choose how many videos you are going to consistently create per month.

Create your first video. Have someone else review it and give you advice on how to make it better.

Create your You Tube account. You will need to have a Gmail account to do this.

Include links from your video to various pages on your website; do not always send them to the home page.

If someone comments on your video, be sure to comment back.

Additional Resources

www.youtube.com – Videos
www.metacafe.com – Videos
www.photobucket.com – Videos, photos
www.vimeo.com – Videos

www.squidoo.com – Articles and videos
www.hubpages.com – Articles and videos
www.examiner.com – Articles and videos; need to commit to submitting 1 to 2 articles/videos per week
www.articlebase.com – Articles and videos
www.gather.com – Articles and videos
www.ezinemark.com – Articles and videos
www.ideamarketers.com – Articles, audios and videos
www.selfgrowth.com – Articles and videos
www.holisticmarketingmentors.com/mastery - Video and article submission and spinning service
www.trafficgeyser.com – Video and article submission service
www.cueprompter.com – Free teleprompter
www.techsmith.com/Camtasia – Excellent video editing software
www.sonycreativesoftware.com/vegassoftware - Video editing software
www.hamstersoft.com/free-video-converter - Video converter software
www.articlevideorobot.com – Converts articles to videos
Kodak Playtouch - Video Camera
Audio Technical lavalier mic - Microphone
Manfrotto tripod 785b – Tripod
Lighting kits – Lighting
www.apple.com - Create presentation slides
www.office.microsoft.com/en-gb/powerpoint - Create presentation slides

www.telestream.net/screen-flow - Create presentation slides

www.adwords.google.com – Keyword tool

MARKETING MASTERY TIP #2

AWESOME Article and Blog Marketing

If videos are not your thing, then writing blogs or articles can give you just as much traction, whether you are posting them on your website or someone else's. You might be asking what is the difference between a blog and an article? Well not much to be honest with you. Typically, a blog is a journal where an article has more facts. Today, these words are used interchangeably.

Start slow; do not try to take on too much at once as article marketing can easily overwhelm people. Write on topics that will engage the audience. Your first paragraph should entice the reader and be keyword rich. Give them great content, so they will want to read your articles in the future or better yet, they will click on your call to action link. Aim for your articles to be between 400 and 500 words. Anything smaller and you will not have enough quality information to interest the reader. If you get much longer than 500 words, you may consider dividing your article into two articles. Remember, attention spans are short these days.

How do you develop content for your articles?

You will want to develop content for your articles the same way you created content for your videos. Write down your ideas in a notebook or keep track of them in Evernote. This way you will not have lapses because you could not think of a topic to write about. Here are some ideas:

Turn your videos into articles.

Answer frequently asked questions and give "how to" instructions.

Give tips to your clients that will help them follow protocols easier.

Give general health and wellness tips.

Use great titles such as – "How to", "Trends", "Top 10".

Focus on making sure your writing is concise and easy to read. You will want to check your Flesch-Kincaid (FK) score for readability. You can easily add this feature to your word documents. See the Additional Resources section for easy download instructions and an excellent article on the Flesch Kincaid score by Michael Masterson. It has been proven that having a FK score below 7.3 will give you higher conversion ratio; meaning more people will read your entire article and are more likely to click on your call to action.

Have a clear purpose for each article you write. What do you want the reader to do next? Make sure this is very clear and you create an easy way for them to do the next step.

See the prior tip on Magnificent Videos for "next step" ideas.

How do you effectively create your blog and articles?

There are tricks to the trade, to help you rank higher in the search engines, so read closely.

First
> The title should contain some of the keywords from your article and should entice the reader to want to know more. Use a headline analyzer tool to determine the emotional value of your title.

Second
> Use a subtitle that re-phrases your title using different keywords.

Third

Keywords should be added throughout the document. Do not overdo it, and use a variety of keyword phrases. Your article must make sense.

Fourth

Either at the bottom of the article or in the resource box includes a call to action that links to a page on your website. This is also your backlink.

You can also use hyperlinks throughout your article. A hyperlink is a keyword that you are using for your website that is hyperlinked to a page on your website. Not only are you getting traction from the backlink but also from the keyword. For example, the keyword could be ADHD coaches. Creating backlinks and hyperlinks are simple. Just highlight the word "ADHD coaches", and then right click your mouse, select hyperlink, type in the website page where you want it directed and click OK. Be careful though some article marketing websites will only allow you to have one or two links created in your article. Make sure you know their guidelines and follow their rules.

Some article writing websites may make you use HTML coding to creating backlinks. If you are not familiar with this do not worry about it. If you have an interest in learning about it, try taking a non-credit course at your local community college or online. This is probably the easiest way to get a basic understanding.

Fifth

In the keyword section, use your best keywords. Make sure you do not guess at these. You will want to do some keyword research first using Google Adwords. The first keyword should be the one in your title and it should also be bolded.

Sixth

Last, but certainly not least you want to let everyone know about the article you just wrote. You can market it in one place or many. However, you will find it more beneficial to market your articles in multiple ways instead of just putting it on your website and hoping people will find it. The whole point of writing is to drive more visitors to your website, add to your list and of course educate the client.

One other nugget of article writing wisdom is to try to post your articles on websites that have a higher Alexa page rank than your website. Alexa rankings were discussed in a prior chapter.

What are some key actions steps you can take?

Choose how many articles/blogs you are going to consistently create per month.

Create your first article/blog. Have someone else

review it and give you advice on how to make it better.

Post your article on Ezine Articles, once you get approval, you can post the article on your own website. You may want to spin the article and post it with a new title to get more visibility from Google. We talk more about this a little later.

Recognize comments on your articles/blog with a prompt response of your own.

How do you maximize the marketing for your article/blog?

Complete the steps below for each article you produce to obtain maximum exposure. Writing lots of articles that are not read by anyone will not do you any good.

Remember, many article submission directories will not accept duplicated content.

Submit your articles <u>in the order</u> described below. Then spin your articles for submission on other websites. You are probably wondering what spinning an article means. Because many sites want unique articles you will want to provide them with slightly different content. This is where spinning articles comes into play. Spinning an article is just rewording the title, first paragraph and a few other sentences throughout the article. There are websites that will do this for you which are listed in the Additional Resources section below. If you decide to use these services, be sure to read the articles after they have been spun checking that the content makes sense and still delivers the intent of your message. Some of these sites may use computers to spin the articles for you and may not provide you with the quality that you want.

First

Submit to ezinearticles.com, even before you publish the article on your website.

Add 5 keywords in the keyword section, the first keyword you list is the keyword in your title. Make sure it is bolded.

Create two powerful resource boxes (for other article submission websites) with calls to action. You will alternate these resource boxes with the articles you write.

Make sure you get approval before publishing your article anywhere else. Approval usually happens 5 to 7 days after submission.

Second

Spin your article. This is where you take your article and make it a little bit different. Change the title, still using keywords. Reword the first paragraph and subtitle along with various other words throughout your article.

Third

Post to your website. Remember, you are posting to ezinearticles.com first.

Post to at least two sites in the Additional Resources section below.

Be sure to spin your article for other sites. This will help you maintain excellent Google rankings.

Fourth

Post your articles on social media sites:
Facebook
Twitter
LinkedIn
Google Plus

Fifth

Post your articles on bookmarking sites:
Stumbleupon

Digg
Delicious
Google Buzz
Technorati

If marketing your articles and videos becomes too overwhelming for you, consider outsourcing these steps to an article or video submission service. Because this is so important to your marketing campaign, this is one of the services we provide our clients at Holistic Marketing Mentors.

Additional Resources

www.ezinearticles.com – Articles
www.squidoo.com – Articles and videos
www.hubpages.com – Articles and videos
www.examiner.com – Articles and videos; need to commit to submitting 1 to 2 articles/videos per week
www.articlebase.com – Articles and videos
www.buzzle.com/authors/become-author.asp - Articles
www.goarticles.com – Articles; minimum of 400 words
www.gather.com – Articles and videos
www.ezinemark.com – Articles and videos
www.brighthub.com – Business and scientific articles
www.ideamarketers.com – Articles, audios and videos
www.selfgrowth.com – Articles and videos
www.helium.com - Articles
www.articlesnatch.com - Articles

www.infobarrel.com – Articles
www.sooperarticles.com - Articles
www.bukisa.com - Articles
www.holisticmarketingmentors.com/mastery - Video and article submission and spinning service
www.trafficgeyser.com – Video and article submission service
www.submityourarticle.com – Article distribution site
www.isnare.com - Article distribution site
www.jetsubmitter.com - Article distribution site
www.articlespinner.org – Sites that will spin articles
www.thebestspinner.com – Sites that will spin articles
www.jetsubmitter.com– Sites that will spin articles
www.uniquearticlespinner.com – Sites that will spin articles
www.aminstitute.com/headline - Headline analyzer tool
www.articlevideorobot.com – Converts articles to videos
www.adwords.google.com – Keyword tool
www.holisticmarketingmentors.com/mastery –Step-by-step instructions to easily install the Flesch-Kincaid reader in Microsoft word
www.awaionline.com/2007/12/clarity-of-your-writing - Michael Masterson's Flesch-Kincaid article

MARKETING MASTERY TIP #3

Your Customer's REAL Hot Buttons

Your customer's hot buttons are the reason why they make the initial appointment with you and buy your services and/or products. These are not always logical reasons but they are extremely important to your business and all aspects of your marketing plan.

So how do you discover their "why"?

Discovering your customer's hot buttons is really quite simple; all you need to do is ask. But do not settle for the first answer. Keep asking until you find the real root cause of their pain. For example, let's say that someone comes to you because he or she has back pain. You might think the answer is obvious. Their hot button is back pain and that may be correct. However, you will not know unless you start asking questions and listen. Ask them directly why they are seeing you. Keep track of the answers and use them in your marketing campaign.

Most practitioners do not use these answers to their advantage and they ask too few of questions. Do not stop with the easy answers. This is where you will find their hot buttons. Here are some common questions you can ask:

Why did you decide to come see me now?

What else did you try?

How is that working for you?

What results did you expect to receive that you did not get?

What did you like about what you tried?

What are you worried will happen if your problem is not solved?

How will your life change if it is solved?

Is there anything else that you think I should know?

Once you understand your client's "why" for seeing you, then you can dig a little deeper. Other questions you will want to get answers to are:

Why did you choose to see me verses someone else for this problem?

What do you expect from your consult?

How long do you think it will take to see results?

What can they expect from you?

What do you require of them so they can see the results they are looking for?

Do not assume you know the answer to these questions. We are all guilty of jumping to conclusions. We ask questions that we think we know the answer to and we do not pay attention to the actual answer itself. Asking questions are essential to making sure not only your marketing is on target but it will also make every other aspect of your business easier.

This discovery process of finding your client's hot buttons is crucial to developing a strong relationship with them. They will not trust you until they know how much you care and truly understand their needs. Yes, you will spend some extra time with them and we know as a wellness practitioner that your time is very valuable. However, the extra time you spend with your new client in this additional discovery process could be the ten minutes that determines whether or not they will be back to see you again. You will use these hot buttons to remind them of why they need to set their next appointment before they leave and why they need to follow your advice exactly as you instruct.

Once you know your customer's hot buttons you can then identify the keywords that you will use in all of your marketing efforts. When you use these hot buttons in your marketing materials your customers know you understand them.

What are some key actions steps you can take?

Make a list of the questions you want to ask your client during your intake evaluation. See the Additional Resources section for a sample questionnaire.

Develop a system for evaluating the answers.

Make a strategy for using these answers in your marketing efforts.

Additional Resources

www.holisticmarketingmentors.com/mastery – Sample client hot button questionnaire

MARKETING MASTERY TIP #4

KINETIC Newspaper, Magazines, Radio and TV

KINETIC Newspaper and Magazines

Many people are intimidated by writing articles for newspapers and magazines. This is a fantastic way for you to become better known as an expert in your industry, especially locally. Your local magazines and newspapers have had many cutbacks over the last few years and are always looking for great content.

How do you become a writer?

For most of us writing takes some practice. It is a matter of picking up the pen and writing. Nevertheless, so many of us get caught up in whether it is good or bad instead of whether we are offering value. Have a friend or relative review it for basic grammatical errors. Most newspapers and magazines will edit the pieces prior to publishing your article.

If you love writing, it is just a matter of contacting some online websites, blogs, magazines and local publishers and asking if you can write for them. Every month they need fresh content, so they need people who want to write and have a message.

These are not marketing pieces, so do not push your services or products. You are providing the reader with great, relevant content that they can use. Try to find something newsworthy or trendy to discuss. Ask if you can offer something free for readers in relation to your article. If this is permitted, then you can include a call to action in the article itself. If this is not allowed, it is still well worth writing these pieces to gain exposure.

As with anything, start small; write pieces for the local "community news" prior to contacting the larger newspaper in your town. Remember to make sure your articles Flesch Kincaid score is below 7.3 and have someone you trust read it for grammatical errors.

The same rule of thumb applies with any writing piece; give great content and make a call to action that links back to your business.

What are some key actions steps you can take?

Pick up every local magazine and newspaper you can find. Places such as doctor's offices and "local" stores always have them.

Pick one magazine or newspaper your ideal client is likely to be reading and contact them to write a column, tips, article, etc.

Look on the Internet and see what online magazines are available for your target market.

Contact one of them and see if they accept content articles from outside authors.

KINETIC Radio & TV

Literally the world is in your hands. You can market your services to anyone on this planet. However, this can sometimes be confusing and overwhelming. The easiest thing you can do is to start local.

There are people in your town that need what you provide. That is why it is imperative to narrow your niche so that you know who to target and what to offer. Remember if you are marketing to the masses you are no different than the majority of people in your profession.

Ask if you can give free tips on a local radio or TV station. This gives you great exposure and experience. Once you have been branded as an expert you can then start to charge for your services or find sponsors.

How do you get your own radio and TV Show?

It is actually not as hard as it seems. Here is how Gail did it.

Gail's Story – For several years, I trained the town of Lancaster for a local race. How did I do it? I actually called the local radio station that sponsored the race and suggested it to them. I was able to answer a key question. Why would it be beneficial to radio station? The answer was that it showed the local community that the radio station cared about getting the town healthy and exposed them to new potential listeners. Each week I gave live updates on the radio. It was a win-win for me, the radio station and the town residents. In the end, I was offered other training program opportunities in the community from my radio exposure. Today I have my own weekly Blog Talk Radio show that is listened to by thousands of people.

Traci agrees that you just have to ask.

Traci's Story – As co-founder of World Wellness Education, I wanted to share other people's healing journeys from sickness to health with a larger audience. I approached the owner of a local radio station and asked if I could interview these people on the radio and have her broadcast it. She agreed. It was very exciting and after the third episode, I approached the local television station and asked if we could do these same interviews on TV. They also agreed. Over the last few years, we have taped over 36 episodes of healing journey interviews and five-minute wellness tips that have been shared with thousands of people all over the country. Because I asked, we have been allowed to educate, inspire and

encourage even more people to live healthier lives, one day at a time, one story at a time.

Another way to get some great press is to offer to people who already have a lot of exposure in the community, your services or products. This works well if people can see a physical transformation such as weight loss because hundreds of people will be asking them how they did it.

Getting out there is instrumental in your success. You just need to approach people and ask. You never know what the answer may be and the exposure you will get.

If you do have a more global audience you can create your own radio show on Blog Talk Radio and publish short TV segments on You Tube.

What are some key actions steps you can take?

Make a list of local radio and TV stations along with contact information.

Look for people you already have relationships with and contact them. If you do not have any contacts, ask around. Someone you know is bound to be able to make an introduction for you.

Make an outline of what you would like to present –
short tips, 30-minute segments, etc.

Make a list of possible sponsors for segments.

Additional Resources

www.holisticmarketingmentors.com/mastery – Step-
by-step instructions to easily install the Flesch-
Kincaid reader in Microsoft word
www.techsmith.com/camtasia – Video, webinar and
audio editing software
www.blogtalkradio.com – Self-radio broadcasting
software
www.youtube.com – You Tube
www.spreaker.com – Online podcasting service
www.itunes.com – Publish podcasts

MARKETING MASTERY TIP #5

EVENTS: Hosting and Sponsoring

Let's first discuss what the difference is between hosting and sponsoring events.

Hosting is when you are the organizer of the event. It may be just you or you may invite others to co-host with you. However, if you organize it, you are the "ring leader" and you get the most exposure. Starting out small is not a bad idea. That way you can test the waters, see what works and what does not and make the necessary changes.

Sponsoring is when you are literally taking part in someone else's venue whether it be live or on the web. You contribute something of value to the program such as education materials, products, time, money, etc. and in return get exposure for your business.

How do you narrow down hosting and sponsorship opportunities?

First and foremost, with both types of events you need to make sure that the event that you are considering has a target market very similar to yours. There is no sense sponsoring an event with firefighters when your target market is women with breast cancer. So be very selective in what events you choose. Do not just throw darts at a board and participate in any event that comes your way.

If you decide to host your own event you will want to give yourself plenty of time to plan and decide who you are going to invite; will you have co-hosts; what you will offer to participants; when and where it will be; and how you will market it to the public.

Make sure you keep good notes so that you can make improvements and have the process be easier the second time you do an event.

How do you market your event?

Marketing your event is important. People will not attend if they do not know what you are doing. Some of the things you can do to increase participation are:

> Put your event on all of the online calendars you can find for your area, as soon as possible.

> Send press releases sixty days out to newspapers, magazines and TV stations on a newsworthy item that will be happening at your event. For example: Are you raising funds for a charity or are you raising awareness for something that has been recently in the news?

Send out save the date notices to your list of clients and potential clients, 45 days out.

Ask newspapers, magazines, radio and TV stations to mention your event with their calendar of events, 45 days ahead and again at two weeks prior to the event.

If the event will be repeated, have a banner or a large sign made that can be displayed across the local streets of your town during the month prior to your event. This is appropriate only if your event is for local participants.

Send out additional information on your event to your list 30 days prior to the event.

Post flyers where your ideal client "hangs out" and hand out postcards about your event 30 days prior to the event.

At about three weeks out, begin creating buzz on social media websites about your event and the different things you are doing that will make it special.

At ten days out create a Facebook event page inviting all of your friends and those that like your Facebook business page.

At ten days out mention the event to your list again along with a link to your Facebook event asking them to share it with their friends and family that may be interested in attending. Also, include relevant tips or articles they may be interested.

Ask the local police department if they will put out electronic signs a few days prior to your event.
The day before the event, send an email to your list and all people on Facebook that said they would attend or maybe attend the event reminding them of the benefits they will receive by going, the fun things that will be happening and the location, date and time of your event.

The day of the event put out several dozen yard signs leading people in from the major access roads to your event. Be sure to pick these up immediately after your event so that you can use them again. Many cities and townships will pick these up and throw them away if they are left out.

Post on your Facebook and Twitter pages that you are excited about the event happening today, along with time and location for them to come out and enjoy the festivities.

Have a contest at the event that people can enter by posting that they are at your event on Facebook, Twitter, Foursquare, etc.

What are some key actions steps you can take?

Look at individuals in your field locally. Where are they participating?

Start asking your target market what events they attend.

Go to your local Chamber of Commerce and get a listing of local events in your area.

Look for local calendars online and see what is happening in your area.

Keep an eye out for upcoming events in your local newspaper.

Brainstorm how you can possibly host your own event with just yourself or a few other key people.

Market your event well using the guidelines mentioned above.

Additional Resources

www.uschamber.com – Chamber of Commerce directory

www.americantowns.com – Local directory of towns

MARKETING MASTERY TIP #6

TAKING the Stage with Confidence

For some, getting on stage is worse than jumping out of an airplane. In fact stage fright ranks up there with the fear of dying.

So why is it that we can say something to one person but when we stand up in front of a group to say the exact same thing fear takes over our entire body? When you think about it that way, it certainly is silly. However, silly or not stage fright is a very real thing.

You can get over your fear of speaking though through baby steps and practice. Speaking on stage is one of the best ways to gain exposure and take your business to the next level.

Ask any entrepreneur; they did not grow their business by being comfortable. Getting out of your comfort zone in any area of your life including personal, client, marketing or business mastery is a step forward in the right direction and speaking is part of it.

How do you take the stage with confidence?

Practice - No speaker is dynamic the very first time.

Prepare

>   Winging it is not a wise idea when you are speaking to a crowd. Write down what you want to say and practice it in front of a mirror or video tape yourself. Once you have it down, shorten it to bullet points that will prompt you when you are on stage.

Focus

>   Get centered and have ritual exercises to bring calm, peace and confidence to your soul. Visualize captivating the audience and clearly delivering your message.

Observe

>   Watch other speakers you admire and take notes. What do they do to keep the audience engaged? How do they summarize their key points? How do they answer questions from the audience?

Learn

>   If you have a fear of speaking or just want to become a better speaker, join a Toastmasters club near you. This will give you the opportunity to practice your speeches in a safe environment while getting encouragement and constructive feedback.

Getting in front of people will not only give you exposure but will also bring you more clients.

However, there are some things you will need to do to ensure success on stage.

The most important thing to remember is that you are being of service to the audience. Give them lots of great information that they can implement into their personal or business lives in bite sized pieces. Do not give them too much information that they leave the presentation feeling overwhelmed and confused.

Your presentation should also do a few things:

> Create trust and connection with the audience.
>
> Show credibility.
>
> Expose vulnerability.
>
> Position your audience; let them know why they should listen to you and what they will learn.
>
> Let them know what your key points will be at the very beginning and then go into more detail throughout your presentation, summarizing your key points at the end.

One of the best ways to explain things is in terms of steps, strategies, tips, techniques or acronyms that can easily be recalled later. You might say, "Today I am going to discuss the five steps to x which are vital to a, b and c in your business." We comprehend information in chunks, so think how you can best teach your audience and have them remember what they have learned.

Each tip/strategy/step should follow the same format:

What is the tip/strategy/step?

Why is it important for them to know about it?

How can it be implemented?

It is important to NOT take questions during your presentation. This changes the energy and you can lose control of the room. It also makes it very difficult to keep focused. Instead, tell the audience at the beginning that you will allow time at the end for any questions they may have regarding your presentation.

If you are allowed or are planning to promote a program or product at the end of your presentation, seed it throughout your talk. You might ask what is seeding? It is giving little nuggets of information throughout your presentation that there is something more that you will be offering your audience at the end. A good rule of thumb is to never seed your program more than two times per main point. This may seem too much for some, so start with where you are comfortable. If you feel like a pushy salesperson, your audience will feel this way also.

The worst thing you can do is at the very end of your presentation blast your audience with some kind of sales pitch when they had no idea it was coming. Many would term this a "hard sell", whereas when programs or products are seeded, the sell at the conclusion can be softer and not as abrasive.

Here are some easy ways you can seed your program or product during your presentation:

> Give them lots of value (tips) and reference that if they want to learn more they can get your product or join your program.

>> Today I will teach you as much as I can in the limited time we have together and before we finish I promise that I will show you how to get more information.

> Have a list of objectives or goals for your presentation. Your last bullet point could be one of the following, which are called transition bullets.

>> And how to take this information from interesting to transformational...

>> And how you can develop your own....

>> And how to get training, sales and support....

>> And how you can craft your own ....

We will give you x number of tips/steps/techniques from our y program.

People who did the y program ….

What inspired me to write the y program is….

Don't worry; I know we have given you a lot of information/content. We have lots of templates, etc. that will support you in our y program.

In our y program/audio number 4, etc., we discuss the 12 ways to a better you, but I want to give you the first two ways with the time we have today.

Allow approximately 5 to 10 minutes for the sale at the end of your presentation, which is enough time to get your point across but not seem too pushy.

What price point should your products be? This is a great question and a general rule of thumb is that for new prospective clients a good price point range for your product/programs is between $97-$497. If they are return clients and have heard you speak before or you are being featured as the keynote speaker you can offer products that range in price from $1500 to well over $10,000.

How do you decrease payment processing issues?

At every venue, especially if multiple speakers are presenting, you run the risk of having problems collecting payments. Here are some sure fire ways to minimize your risks:

Check your order forms very carefully. Compare everything with their physical credit card.

Process the order as fast as possible; right then and there if you can. In today's world, you can swipe the card with an attachment to your cell phone, or even enter it on your phone or computer for a very small transaction fee and no monthly fees. See the Additional Resources section below for suggestions.

Send them an immediate email after payment and give them something to do so they see that they are getting something for their money right away. Explain in the email the benefits of what they just purchased.

Do not forget to grow your list.

When speaking, be sure you get as many contacts in the room as possible. So many people speak in front of their target market and totally forget about getting their contact information. Here are some easy ways to do this:

> Before the event, ask the promoter if they can give you a list of the attendees with their email addresses. Send them a thank you email after your presentation with an opt-in form that will give them something free. You do not want to just add people to a list without them approving it otherwise you will be considered a spammer.

> Have a sign up list to get your newsletter/tips, etc. on your table.

> Hold a drawing for a grand prize but state on the bowl that everyone wins because they will get a free subscription to your newsletter/tips, etc.

> Host a teleclass or webinar a week after your presentation on a particular topic. Have them sign up at the back of the room to gain access to the call in information.

> Get their cell phone number and text them with a way to opt-in to your list right at the conference.

> Hold a contest for people to like your Facebook page while at the conference and if they make a comment on your Facebook page they automatically win something.

What are some key actions steps you can take?

Join Toastmasters; this is a must to gain experience and confidence.

If you think that you have some basic speaking skills, then begin to prepare a signature talk that can be used in a variety of settings.

Decide what equipment, if any, you will need during your speaking engagements such as a projector, screen, extension cords, microphones, laptops, etc.

Once you feel confident, contact one place a week where you can possibly speak.

Plan exactly how you are going to get leads and act upon them.

If you can sell products or services decide what these will be and how they will be packaged and sold.

Decide how you will be taking payments.

Try to have someone video tape your presentations if possible. These can then be used to help you become a better speaker and when you produce something really great, you can also use it as a standalone product. If you can't get someone to video tape your presentation, use a small voice recorder that you can attach to your jacket or top.

Additional Resources

www.toastmasters.org – Find a Toastmasters Club near you

www.apple.com/uk/iwork/keynote - Create presentation slides

www.office.microsoft.com/en-gb/powerpoint - Create presentation slides

www.telestream.net/screen-flow - Create presentation slides

www. intuit-gopayment.com – Low cost credit card processing

www.squareup.com – Low cost credit card processing

www.amazon.com – San Disk mini recorder

MARKETING MASTERY TIP #7

IMPACTFUL Social Media

You can look at this as an opportunity or as a curse. For many, it is overwhelming and they do not do anything or they do it for a while and give up. Yet, if you use social media correctly, it can help you form a devoted group of followers and even establish some great business relationships.

If you find it too overwhelming or you just hate doing it perhaps think about outsourcing it. However, be careful because if you are not writing the material your brand and voice can be altered.

The most important thing to learn is if you want to stay connected with your clients and potential customers you need to have a presence on social media. Current social media sites that will give you exposure to your ideal clients are Facebook, Twitter, YouTube, LinkedIn, Google+ and Pinterest.

Facebook alone has over 800,000,000 users and this is always growing.

Pinterest is the fastest growing site using social media and is also the fastest growing site in Internet history. This is where your clients are hanging out and therefore you should consider hanging out there also.

How do you make your social media impactful?

One piece of advice is to put the customer first. Give them lots of value, love and content. The worst thing someone can do on social media is constantly promote themselves, their products or someone else's stuff. It puts a bad taste in people's mouths.

There are a few things that can catapult your social media experience.

Remember the 25-30% rule. Only promote something every three to four posts. Give them a tip, a quote, make comments or link back to educational articles (perhaps your own blog). After this, you can offer them something of value. If you are posting a lot of posts each week, you will probably want to limit your special offers even more. You may want to only ask your audience to purchase something or do something once a week so that you do not to turn people off.

Use a social media loading platform such as Hootsuite. It will take a huge load off your shoulders. Yes, a little impersonal, but it does save a lot of time and it will help keep your sanity.
Last, if social media is going to set you off the deep end start with the media site that you think will give you the biggest bang for your buck. Learn it for a few months then add something else.

We believe that this is a key ingredient to attracting and retaining more clients to your business. That is why we have begun offering completely done for you services at Holistic Marketing Mentors for all of your social media needs.

It is just a fact. The more value you give to your customers in a variety of platforms, the more they will respect you as an authority. The more they "see you"; the more they "trust you".

What are some key actions steps you can take?

Start with one platform; learn it, build a following, and become consistent before you move to another platform.

Outsource the setup and maintenance of your platforms, if needed.

Use Hootsuite to schedule your posts.

Choose a professional picture or something that represents you well. Do not put a crazy picture up unless that is how you want to be represented to the world.

Additional Resources

www.facebook.com - Facebook
www.twitter.com - Twitter
www.linkedin.com – LinkedIn (networking for
business professionals)
www.plus.google.com – Google+
www.pinterest.com - Pinterest
www.hootsuite.com – Schedule posts on all
platforms in advance
www.tweetadder.com – Add followers and follow
back people on Twitter
www.holisticmarketingmentors.com/mastery - Step
by step instructions on how to use social media
effectively
www.holisticmarketingmentors.com/mastery - Done
for you social media setup and maintenance of
accounts

MARKETING MASTERY TIP #8

NICHE Marketing

Now that you know your ideal customer, it is time to market to your niche. There is no right or wrong way and with much of this, it is a matter of trial and error. Some things will work really well and others you will need to take off your list.

How do you market to your niche?

First, find out where your customers hang out. We have talked about where they are hanging out online but you also need to know where your customer hangs out locally. These businesses already have your customer base. Did you get that? They already have your customer base in a physical body, an address, email, phone number etc. So use it to your advantage. Your success depends on your ability to reach your target market effectively in the quickest amount of time.

Sit down with the places of business where your customers visit or perhaps schedule a phone call with them. Establish a rapport and find out how you can best help support them and their business. Then make a plan of how you can work together. The worst thing you can do is go into the meeting only one sided and expecting them to give you everything.

Here are some potential ideas to keep in mind:

Establish a friendly referral relationship.

Do a joint venture program together where you both are contributing something.

Offer to write a section in their newsletter.

Offer to do a special event at their location for free.

Sponsor a giveaway for their clients.

Establish a friendly competition.

The list goes on and on and the only thing limiting you is getting out there.

What are some key actions steps you can take?

Make a list of where you customer's hang out.

Commit to contacting one to three places a week via phone.

Commit to scheduling a convenient time to talk on the phone or meet for coffee.

Make a plan of action to move forward.

Follow through with your promises; your integrity is something you cannot afford to lose.

> *Dr. Ann's Story - Dr. Ann is a Naturopath and when asked about her specialty, her answer was "everyone." She soon realized being a "generalist" may not be the best thing for marketing her practice. After taking a look at her passion and her successes, she noticed that she had great success with fertility patients. She currently is in the process of designing an intensive program which will include several different package options. Dr. Ann saw the opportunity to not only help more people, but also bring in additional revenues without working so hard. She found that marketing herself as the infertility specialist allows her to work with more of her favorite types of patients.*

Additional Resources

The Answer by John Assaraf and Murray Smith
www.holisticmarketingmentors.com/mastery - FREE report on What Your Customer's Really Want

MARKETING MASTERY TIP #9

GENIUS Business Cards & Networking

GENIUS Business Cards

Have you ever gone to a networking event and collected lots of business cards, only to get back to the office and wonder who they were or why you even took their card in the first place? It has happened to everyone.

Your business card should be considered a sales tool. It is something that someone should look at and understand what you do and what you can offer them instantaneously in clear terms.

Most important, it should give them a reason to talk to you at a future date. You want people to take action with your business card. Your ideal prospect should say, wow, I need you!

If you really want to stand out above the crowd, give them something other than a business card such as a CD or a 5x7 card with your business information.

How do you make business cards attractive?

This is what should be on your business card to attract potential customers.

<u>Front of your card:</u>
Name
Tagline- optional, but if you use it, use it on everything
Ways to reach you – office, cell, email
Picture – so they remember you

<u>Back of your card:</u>
Questions – this self qualifies them and helps them describe what you do clearly and effectively to other people
A call to action – have them go to your website for a free gift; call you for a consult, etc.

What are some key actions steps you can take?

Order business cards in smaller quantities so that you can change them more often with different calls to action, pictures, etc.

Take other's individual business cards only if you are truly interested in what they have to offer.

Take notes on the back of business cards so you remember what you were going to do next with them.
Get a matte finish on at least one side, so people can take notes on yours.

Follow up within 24 hours of taking someone's business card. Most people do not do this, this alone will make you stand out above your peers, and you will reap the benefits.

Additional Resources

www.gotprint.com – Online printing
www.vistaprint.com – Online printing

GENIUS Networking

We have all gone to networking events, where you stare at each other, stand in the corner or say the typical line, what do you do? It is often awkward and uncomfortable. It is unfortunate that people are taking the time to "try" and grow their businesses but are not being effective doing it. Networking events can generate a great deal of business if you follow a few simple rules of etiquette.

Behave as if you are the host or hostess. Get there early and position yourself to where you can greet people as they arrive.

The most important rule is to be genuinely interested in the other person. Do not brag about what you do and how wonderful you are.

Another golden rule is to listen. Do not focus on what you need to do when you leave the event or the next thing you want to say. Just relax and enjoy the conversation. Find out about their background and how they got into business; be curious.

The following are some questions you can ask that will help you get to know the person you are talking to so that you can understand what they do and to be able to refer business to them:

What motivated you to be in this business?

How long have you been doing this?

Who is your ideal client or niche?

What services do you offer?

What makes you unique from others in your industry?

Do you have employees or subcontractors?

What skill sets do you feel you excel in?

What is your goal for the next year?

How can I help you?

At the end, make sure you reflect and think about future opportunities you might have with this person. Can you help them grow their business? Do they have contacts they might be able to connect with you? Are there areas that you might be able to collaborate?

Be sure to ask them how you can best support them in their business. Can you see how a person can start to warm up to you with these simple networking strategies?

Did you notice there was no mention of how you can sell them a service or a product? When you focus more on helping others rather than the actual sale, you will find yourself in the flow and the sales will begin to happen. In addition, networking events will become much more enjoyable and less stressful.

Too many of us focus on the sale way too early in the process. Instead learn to focus on building relationships.

Be strategic in selecting the networking events that you are attending. Try it once and if it is not a good fit move on. Do not keep pounding your head in the sand.

Last, when you commit to attending an event, try and get the list of individuals that are attending prior to the event so you can set up a strategy for who you would like to meet.

How can you engage people in your business?

Most people when asked will say something to the order of, "Hi, I am Sally Jones and my business is ABC Company. We help people with nutrition and weight loss."

This example is actually a little better than most because at least she said how she helps people. So often you do not even know what the business does.

Creating an effective quick commercial or elevator speech takes some time and practice. Do not think you are going to walk into a networking event this evening and have this nailed down. You need to gauge people's responses and make changes.

Here is a good basic example:

I work with x, who struggle with y, and would like to z. What separates my service from other health professionals is c and because of this, clients are able to d. Right now we are offering a free b for everyone who likes our d Facebook page.

This basic introduction really lets the person know whether they or someone they know may need your services. It also has a very simple and clear call to action that you should change often. Remember, you are not selling anything. At this stage, you are only building relationships and offering items or information of value.

What are some key actions steps you can take?

Get out there – find networking events in your area.

Make a list and put the meetings on your calendar.

Be consistent about attending the events you like; remember this is about building relationships.

Develop a short elevator speech. Measure its effectiveness and change it as necessary.

Think of several calls to action.

Additional Resources

www.uschamber.com – Chamber of Commerce Directory
www.networkingforprofessionals.com – Networking for Professionals
www.bni.com – Business Network International

www.tangerinenetworkinggroup.com – Tangerine Networking Group

www.woamtec.com – Women On a Mission to Earn Commission

www.nafe.com – National Association of Female Executives

www.wen-usa.com – Women's Entrepreneur Network

www.ewomennetwork.com – E-Women Network

SELF MASTERY

When you start running your own business you might feel that you must work 12 to 16 hour days; six to seven days a week. You forget about vacations because who will see your clients or take care of your customers if you are not there? Before you know it, you are pulling your hair out and working yourself sick.

Have you ever told a client, how can you take care of others, if you do not take care of yourself? We want you to ask yourself this same question. Yes taking care of your business is important but if you are not taking care of yourself you are no good to anyone.

So how do you take care of yourself, your business and your clients at the same time? You do this through Self Mastery.

SELF MASTERY TIP #1

MINDSET

In school, we were told what to think and what to know. Rarely did we ever hear anything about how to think and how to use our mind to achieve our dreams. We hope that you understand that your mindset ultimately leads you to your success or failure. Your mindset controls every action you take, in every aspect of your life.

Have you ever noticed that some people can build business after business with some degree of success; while others never get their businesses off the ground? You could say that the successful entrepreneurs had the financing or even support from others to achieve their dreams. However, if these entrepreneurs were not in their right mind, they would not have attracted individuals to invest in them, nor would have they received whole heartedly the support from others. They would not have known what actions steps were the right ones and which opportunities to focus upon.

The mind has been studied for centuries and most recently with the shifting of our planet's energy people are starting to wake up to their amazing individual power. In fact some advanced researchers are discovering that mindset might be the first thing that affects the genetic make-up of a cell. For

example if someone has breast cancer and they
believe they got it because their mother had it,
researchers are discovering that this likely had a
direct impact on the disruption of the cells.
You can ask the same thing about businesses that
fail and businesses that succeed. Do businesses fail
or succeed because of outside circumstances like the
economy or because of internal circumstances
caused by our mindset? Let's get into this a little
deeper.

How do you have an expanded mindset?

First, look at your belief systems and change the
ones that do not serve you. We discuss this in great
detail because your beliefs about a situation play a
huge role in your outcome. If you believe you can
do it, you can. If you believe you cannot, you will
not.

How do you see your reflection? Is it distorted in the
ripples of a wave? Is it clear as in a quiet body of
water? Is it completely opposite when looking in a
mirror? How you see yourself in relation to your
world predicts how you will behave and perform in
your daily routines.

An example of this is if you view your body as the
perfect vessel than you will treat your body as such.
You will provide your perfect body with perfect
nutrition and the right amount of exercise.

If you believe you deserve success you will take actions to ensure your success. If you believe you will fail than you will take actions that will lead to your failure. It is when you think of yourself as "less than" that you do things that will create roadblocks on your highway to success.

You create more of whatever you focus upon. If you think that people around you are rude and uncaring than that is what you will see. If you think that people do not care about their health or will not spend money to stay well, than this is how the people in your world will behave. As Jennifer Hough says, "what you ooze and what you be has everything to do with what you are attracting into your life." However, if you change your perception and believe that the people around you are caring and helpful than that is what you will see.

If you are experiencing the same problems repeatedly try looking at your life through a different set of glasses by putting a different spin on things. What do you have to lose? Chances are your problem will become less of one and eventually will be eliminated.

You must change your view of yourself and your view of those around you in order to change your life. Start small with one person or one item that you want to perceive differently. Remember that you are changing only your perception of the situation not the person or situation itself.

For example, let's say you are stuck in traffic on the freeway. No one is moving but you see this car coming from behind you down the right side of the road. You get mad and frustrated because this person is breaking the law. They should have to wait in traffic just like everyone else! Who do they think they are?

Now, how would your perception change if you knew there was a little boy in the back seat that was bleeding profusely from his arm and may not make it to the hospital alive if his Dad does not break the law and drive down the side of the freeway? We often do not know why people behave the way they do. Do not take their actions personally.

Start observing your thoughts and how you truly perceive things and others. When you change your perceptions, you change how you feel about yourself and the world around you. When you change how you feel and what you focus on, you change the events that happen in your life.

What are some action steps you can take?

List your current beliefs about your life and your business.

Work on creating new belief systems to replace those that do not serve you.

Pay attention to your inner voice.

Observe your thoughts.

Focus more on what you want and less on what you do not want.

Carol's & Bruce's Stories- Carol is an acupuncturist and when she first set up her practice she felt inexperienced and therefore should charge less than other acupuncturists in her city. Her fees were about 20% less than some of her peers.

Bruce also started his acupuncture practice at the same time about 5 minutes down the road from Carol. However, Bruce was confident in his abilities and from the very beginning began charging the standard fees.

About 6 months after they were both in business Bruce and Carol ran into each other at a bookstore. Recognizing each other from school, they sat down to have a cup of coffee and to talk about life in the real world. Through this conversation, Carol realized that Bruce was doing quite a bit better than she was. He not only was bringing in more money per patient but also had a significant number of more clients than she did.

What Bruce told Carol that day changed her life forever. He said, "Carol, when you charge less for your time, you are actually subconsciously telling your patients and everyone else that you do not feel comfortable with your abilities as a healer. Your patients feel this on some level and because they are desperate to get better, they come to me or someone else because they want to be confident that they are going to be healed. This will not change until you change. You are actually probably one of the best acupuncturists that I know, but your business is not going to reflect your true abilities until you accept them yourself."

Carol pondered what Bruce told her the rest of the week and on Monday, she made a change. She increased her fees and within weeks, she noticed an increase in patients. Today, Carol's fees have increased to among the highest in her city and she enjoys a full schedule. The only thing that changed for Carol was her mindset. She perceived her worth differently and she was able to move forward and have a successful practice because of her new perception.

Additional Resources

Wishes Fulfilled by Wayne Dyer
Flip the Switch by PJ McClure
Wired for Success, Programmed for Failure by James B. Richards
The One-Minute Millionaire: The Enlightened Way to Wealth by Mark Victor Hansen and Robert G. Allen

SELF MASTERY TIP #2

Be AUTHENTIC, Be Real

Be yourself! This seems so basic. Yet most of us focus too much of our time on who everyone else wants us to be and we forget who we really are. We feel we have to be the perfect healer, parent, child, etc.

Does any of this sound familiar? Ask yourself, do you know anyone who is perfect or has anything that is perfect? This is actually a trick question because no one is "perfect". We all make mistakes. Please understand it is okay to make mistakes. Mistakes just shine the light on areas of opportunity.

Why is being authentic so important? It is important because when you try to pretend that you do not make mistakes or that nothing in your life can be improved upon, people know that you are LYING. When you lie to your clients they instinctively feel this and they have difficulties trusting you. If your customer does not trust you they will not be compliant, nor will they refer you. Eventually they will stop seeing you all together.

How do you be authentic?

Be honest with yourself and with others. This is not to say that you need to lay it all out on the table and tell your clients all of your dirty little secrets. It just means to show them glimpses of the "true" you. If they ask you how is business? Do not say, I am worried I will stay in business because I have very few clients. Instead, say, I am always looking for new clients. If you know of anyone who can use my services, will you refer them to me? People love to help others and if you ask them to, they will help you.

You will also want to be specific with what type of client you are looking for. For instance, are you looking to help new moms lose their baby weight? Do you love helping people get rid of migraines? The more specific you are the more likely you will be able to set yourself apart from your peers. Now when your clients ask you how business is you can say, I am seeing great success with helping people eliminate migraines once and for all; if you know of someone who suffers from chronic headaches or migraines will you refer me? If they say yes, which they will, give them a few extra business cards – have them put their name on the back of the card when they give them out. This way you know who to thank for the referrals sent your way.

Always remember why you got into your business in the first place. Your goal is to make people feel better during every encounter they have with you. John C. Maxwell said, "People, don't care about what you know, until they know how much you care."

Therefore, before you add new products and/or services take a look and see what you can do to improve your client experience.

Do not be afraid to tell someone that you do not know the answer by making something up and trying to bluff your way through it. Your clients will respect you more if you tell them that you do not know but you will get back to them after you have done some research. Then be sure to keep your word and do the research promptly and give them the answer.

That leads us into doing what you say you are going to do. How many times has someone told you they would do something and they never followed through? What did you think afterwards? We know this is difficult and we have all failed at follow through at some time or another. The point here is to take your word seriously and do your very best to have a system in place so that you will not forget to keep your word. A great resource is the Get It Done application. You can send a quick email to your Get it Done account with the task as the subject line and you never have to worry about losing your note or you can just enter the task quickly on many smart phones.

What are some action steps you can take?

Be honest with yourself and with others.

Show every customer how much you care every time you encounter them.

If you do not know something say so.

Have a system in place so that if you tell someone that you will do something you have a note to do it.

Additional Resources

www.getitdoneapp.com - To do lists

SELF MASTERY TIP #3

STOPPING Limiting Beliefs and Self Sabotage

STOPPING Limiting Beliefs

Why do you get so close to your goals yet often fall short? Why do you struggle doing the tasks that you need to do in order to achieve your goals?

To obtain the life you really want you need to change who you really are! You need to remove limiting beliefs. This can be somewhat scary. You have probably heard someone say, I am what I am or this is who I am and I cannot change. Well these are just excuses and if you want to be in this same spot five years from now just keep believing them. If you really want a different outcome, then it is time you make some real and everlasting changes.

You can change who you are, you have done it many times in your life already. When you were younger you were a student who may have focused on school, sports or your social life. As you grew older you changed your focus. You started to work and maybe had a family. In each of these areas in your life you became someone else. In fact, many people are one person at work, someone different with their family and somebody else entirely with their friends.

How do you stop limiting beliefs?

So let us look at your business and how you can remove these limiting beliefs once and for all. Take a few minutes to answer the following questions.

What do I really want?

Why do I really want this?

How will my life change because of wanting this?

Do I really want my life to change in these ways?

If you answered "yes" to the last question then you can move on to the next paragraph. If you answered "no", then you need to look at changing what you want. There is no reason for you to try to achieve a goal that is going to affect areas of your life in what you perceive to be a negative manner. Once you are clear on what you want, why you want it and how your life will change for the better than you are ready to move on to the next steps in manifesting your dreams.

Take a sheet of paper and write whatever comes to mind when answering the following questions.

As a person who has x goal, I currently do the following tasks on a regular basis to achieve this goal.

As a person who has x goal, I currently feel the following as I am completing tasks to achieve this goal.

There are very few things that have not already been achieved by someone else. Take a look around you; go to the library or do a Google search. Someone somewhere has achieved what you are wanting in your life.

Who has already accomplished what you want to do?

What do you think they did to reach this goal? Answer as many questions below as you can.

What time did they wake up?

How did they dress?

What did they do?

Whom did they call?

What appointments did they make?

What paperwork did they do?
Were they confident when they talked with others?

Did they believe in themselves?

How often did they practice their skill sets?

What did they eat?

When did they go to sleep?

What support people did they have in their lives (friends, coaches, mentors, family)?

How do you think they felt as they were working on their goal?

How do you think they felt once they achieved their goal?

Notice these questions are asking you what you think. Through your research, you will have the answer to some of these questions but definitely not all of them. Do not get caught up trying to make this perfect. Otherwise, you will just create an excuse on why you cannot move forward towards your success. Trust your intuition and try to imagine exactly what you think this person was doing and feeling. Be sure to write all of this down. It will be important for you to review this as you are moving forward on your journey.

You are an incredible human being and you have access to all of the universal knowledge that everyone else does. You can accomplish anything you set your mind to. The key is setting your mind to accomplishing it. Instead of setting your mind to just doing what you have always been doing, it is time to change who you are. Take the answers to the last set of questions and visualize yourself as that person.

Visualize yourself as being someone who has already accomplished your goal.

Visualize what you did to reach this goal.
Visualize what you did to celebrate the occasion.

Try to use all of your senses in this exercise. What do you smell? What do you hear? How do you feel? What do you see? What do you taste?

You can achieve anything you would like to if you are determined enough to develop the skill sets required to accomplish it. Try not to put a time limit on your dream. Time is not relative to the act of manifesting our dreams and goals.

Everything will happen at the appropriate time. Your job is just to keep developing the next skill set so that you can accomplish the next task. If you keep moving forward in this manner you will always find the pot of gold at the end of your rainbow.

What are some action steps you can take?

Answer the questions above.

Create the visualization suggested; be as detailed as possible.

Additional Resources

www.thevitalyou.com – Get Out of Your Own Way Program
www.theiameffect.com Harrison Klein "I Am" program
www.askandreceive.org - Ask and Receive Technique by Pat Carrington

STOPPING Self-Sabotage

Self-sabotage is another way of limiting yourself and can lead to self-destruction. It can be anything from eating and exercise habits to business and relationships.

For example:

Have you ever started a diet and lost a few pounds just to put the weight back on a week later?

Have you ever joined the gym with great intentions and then within two months no longer even stepped inside it?

Have you ever used affirmations and got frustrated because the changes were slower than anticipated?

Have you ever felt like you were taking three steps forward and two steps back in your business?

Many feel that if you work extra hard you will get what you want out of life. The fact is the vast majority of the population is always wanting something more and achieving their goals never satisfies them.

Unfortunately, too many business failures are due to the owner self-sabotaging themselves. Here are some examples:

You have a goal of making an extra $2,000 a month, yet you spend two hours every day on Facebook chatting with your friends or playing games.

You know networking is a means of finding new customers but you find every excuse not to attend events or when you do attend events you talk to only people you know.

Even though there are thousands of ways we unconsciously self-sabotage ourselves we can stop it. It is possible to allow ourselves to be successful and achieve our dreams.

How do you stop self-sabotaging yourself and your business?

Areas of neglect can come back to haunt you. Self-sabotage may be a sign that there is a blockage that needs to be addressed. This may bring up a lot of fear for you. Fear is not what is stopping your success; hiding in fear is what is stopping your success. Shedding light on your fears enables you to move forward.

Look for areas in your life that are filled with procrastination. These will give you clues as to where you may be hiding out in fear. The longer you delay doing something because of procrastination the more stress and worry you will have in your life. Quit worrying and procrastinating and just do it.

Your mind responds to your feelings and your feelings are a result of your beliefs. If you are having roadblocks in setting and achieving your goals your beliefs may be the problem. It is important that your belief systems be in alignment with your goals. If not you will continue unconsciously self-sabotaging yourself.

When setting a goal pay close attention to how you feel. Do you feel anxious, nervous or overwhelmed?

These are clues that your beliefs are not in alignment with your goal.

Fears challenge your beliefs. This is a wonderful opportunity to get to know yourself better and find out what is preventing you from moving forward. Ask yourself, what am I feeling? Keep asking and you will come up with many different things.

One great way of getting to the root of your issue is to keep chunking it down. Keep asking yourself, what you are feeling and how that emotion makes you feel. For example: perhaps you are feeling anxious; being anxious makes you feel sad; feeling sad makes you feel hopeless; and feeling hopeless makes you feel anxious. When you start repeating the same emotional phrases you have most likely reached the root issue. This exercise is often very eye opening.

Another form of self-sabotage is complaining. Everything we complain about is an unconscious intention to produce those results. What you focus on is what you attract into your life. Many of us do not love ourselves. We feel like we are undeserving. When we say, I am fat or I am not seeing enough clients. We are just creating more of this.
Do not lie to yourself and say, I feel thin if you truly do not feel that way. However, you can ask yourself, what it would feel like to feel thin? What would it feel like to have your body feel healthy all over?

What would it feel like to have your calendar full of clients that pay on time, follow your directions and refer tons of people to you?

Now you that you are aware of how you are self-sabotaging yourself you can look at your dream and see it with fresh eyes. When you begin to feel scared or anxious you can take a deep breath and reassure yourself that it is okay. You now have a new understanding and can move forward toward your desires without the roadblocks of the past.

Understand that your mind may be trying to warn you of possible dangers up ahead because it is experiencing something new. Reassure yourself that you are okay; you know where you are going and even if things go wrong they will not be any worse than if you continue to stay stuck.

Finally, look for opportunities not obstacles. Instead of asking why it cannot be done, ask how it can be done. A great example of this is writing this book in just 30 days. It was a challenge given to over 50 people in a seminar. We could have just dismissed the challenge or we could have looked at it as an opportunity. We chose to look at it as an opportunity that would allow us to give you the very best of ourselves and not make you wait years before we finally got around to it. If we had allowed a year to write the book, it would have taken a year. Your project will always take as long as you allow it to. Instead we chose to have laser focus and did what many said was impossible in just one month. Just a side note, we did allow another 30 days for editing and publishing.

What are some action steps you can take?

Write down your goals and notice how you feel about each goal.

Explore these feelings deeper, ask yourself questions like:

Why do I continue to do things that are not in my best interest?

How do I break this cycle?

How can I change my feelings to better this situation?

What small thing can I do daily that will help me achieve this goal?

What skill sets can I learn to help me?

Who can I look to outsource some items that will help me reach my goal quicker?

Who can serve me as a mentor or coach?

Join a mastermind group to help you brainstorm and bust past barriers quickly.

Additional Resources

www.holisticmarketingmentors.com/mastery - Reach your goals every time
www.holisticmarketingmentors.com/mastery - Mastermind groups
Natural Brilliance by Paul R. Scheele
Psycho-Cybernetics Updated and Revised by Maxwell Maltz and Dan Kennedy

SELF MASTERY TIP #4

THANKFULNESS

Why is it that we live a society where we are always looking for what we do not have instead of being grateful for what we do have?

Take a look at your own life. Are you always striving for something better and not being thankful for what you have in the present moment?

Third world countries often have much less than what we have and yet are more grateful. They are thankful they are alive, have shelter and something to eat. Yet many of us take this for granted.

Appreciating everything in your life and living in the present are two important elements in seeing more of what you want appear in your life. It is as if 'source' is saying, if you cannot appreciate what I have given you, why should I give you more? Being thankful brings more joy into your life. When you feel joy in what you do you are not tired, bored, stuck, angry, fearful or sad.

How to remember to be thankful?

Every time you get a client, a check, new shoes, food at the grocery store, take a moment and be grateful. It does not have to be anything extensive, but it is the mere fact of acknowledging that you are thankful for what you have in this beautiful world.

At night when you are sharing a meal with family or friends share something you are grateful for that day.

Start a daily gratitude journal; try writing something new each day. You will be amazed at how your outlook on life will change and how great you will start perceiving your life to be.

What are some key actions steps you can take?

Recognize your own internal and external dialogue. Are you grateful or resentful? Are you whining and complaining or are you seeing opportunities?

Share with others things you are thankful for.

Start a gratitude journal. Take time to reflect each day.

Additional Resources

Excuse Me Your Life is Waiting Playbook by Lynn Grabhorn

SELF MASTERY TIP #5

EXECUTING the Law of Attraction

You need to realize that the Law of Attraction is ALWAYS working in your life. If your life is good and is filled with things and people that you want than at some level of your being you understand how the Law of Attraction works.

If you are experiencing difficulties and are feeling a lot of lack than most likely you are unconsciously drawing these things into your life. If you are stuck at a certain income level and cannot get beyond that imaginary ceiling it is because this is where you unconsciously feel you belong.

Whether your life is good or your life could be better we want you to understand how to consciously create the life of your dreams. Your dreams can become reality. If you dream it, you can achieve it.

How do you magnetize the Law of Attraction and have it work for you?

There are many books written on this subject and we give you several that we like in our Additional Resources section. Our goal with this chapter though is to share with you what is typically missing when most people try to apply the Law of Attraction in their lives.

We hear way too often from people that they have tried to apply the Law of Attraction principles but that they do not work. We want to show you how you can take what you already know on this subject and have it consciously work in your life every time.

Our feelings are what make the Law of Attraction happen.

Life is really about your journey; practice enjoying living in the moment. Your journey is what is important not anyone else's. It is what YOU think that is important because your entire life's experiences are based off your thoughts and your feelings around your thoughts.

So many of us focus on the future; we will be happy when this happens; we will be successful when this happens; we can rest when this happens. At other times, we live in the past worried about something we did or did not do. Try to make every effort not to live in the regrets of the past or the hopes of the future.

Focus on finding the joy and passion in what you are doing at all times. Find your happiness in the present moment and watch how this leads from one incredible moment to the next. Finding joy in everything you do will lead you to greater success than you have even imagined.

Practice gratitude or find a way to make an unpleasant task enjoyable. For example, listen to music or books on your .mp3 player as you do monotonous chores around the office or house.

If you cannot find joy in what you are doing then find someone else to do the project for you. It will not serve you to hold on to the task waiting for a better time or more money to come into your life. Remember it is your feelings behind a project that will determine its success. If you do things begrudgingly, dragging your feet and hating every minute of it, then this will show in the results; find the joy or delegate the task!

Your heart emits the perfect frequency for manifestation when you are filled with joy and gratitude. You need to do more than just think about what you want your life to look like; you need to also feel it.

When you feel joy in what you are doing you are co-creating with source. Manifestation requires patience; the seed is planted and you wait for it to grow. Manifesting is the power to make your dreams come true. When you trust that life will provide you with what you need, you act as co-creator with the universe.

John Assaraf reminds us, "You have the genius within you to achieve all your goals." What would your life look like if you could not fail? What would your life look like if you could do everything right? Feel it! Experience it! Be it! Always look for ways to have more happiness, more peace, and more joy in your life. Quit waiting to live your dream, begin living today as if it has already materialized.

Write out your vision in detail and create a mind movie or vision board to look at daily. You can create a mind movie by using a software program that allows you to upload pictures of your goals. You also insert affirmations that will help you along your journey and even add music. You can play your mind movie in the background on your computer creating subliminal messages as you go about your daily work.

Vision boards are similar to a mind movie except they are usually created using poster board with pictures of all your goals, affirmations and anything else that will help you visualize what you want your life to be like.

When you are reviewing what you want your life to look like you need to feel it. What do your dreams feel like, what do they taste like, what do you hear, what do you see, and what do you smell? When you do this on a daily basis you will begin to see doors open around you that will lead you to your most amazing dreams.

This is not about sitting on the couch and attracting what you want. The Law of Attraction works because you either attract to you the steps to realize your dreams or you attract to you the steps to realize your worries.

Abraham says, "The Universe does not know or care whether the vibration that you are offering is in response to something you are living right now and observing, or in response to something you are imagining. In either case, the Universe accepts it as your point of attraction and matches it."

When you are creating your vision put everything as "I am" not "I will". If your dream is in a future tense it will always be something in your future and you will have difficulties creating this in your present reality.

Remember if you dream it you can achieve it. However, the key here is - you have to also believe it. Does it feel natural? Does it feel right? If it does not feel believable or when worry overwhelms you, ask yourself instead what would this situation look like if I did not need to worry about it? What would it look like for this dream to feel natural, for it to feel perfect?

What are some action steps you can take?

Pay attention to what you are thinking.

Make a conscious decision to find more joy, happiness and passion in your life.

Take some time and answer some of the questions above. Keep them handy and continue asking.

Create a vision board, write out your vision or create a mind movie.

Regularly focus on your dreams and how it fills to accomplish them.

When worry overwhelms you, ask yourself what the situation would look and feel like if you did not need to worry? If everything was perfect, what would it look and feel like?

Additional Resources

www.worldwellnesseducation.org/harrison-klein-2 - Traci Brosman interviewing renown transformationalist Harrison Klein on Creating Lasting Joy
Manifest Your Destiny by Wayne Dyer
Law of Attraction by Esther and Jerry Hicks
The Law of Attraction by Michael J. Losier
The Power by Rhonda Byrne
www.mindmovies.com - Create a mind movie
www.mydesktoptherapist.com - Subliminal mind movie software

SELF MASTERY TIP #6

REMOVING Feelings of Being Overwhelmed

With so many tasks needing to be done in your business it is easy to become overwhelmed. When overwhelmed you can become paralyzed and then instead of accomplishing even small amounts of the tasks at hand you get nothing done. You turn to other emotional comforts instead like watching too much TV, playing on Facebook, eating too much, sleeping too much, drinking too much, etc.

In today's world it can be extremely difficult to find that perfect balance. There is often less time for family, exercise, meditation and taking care of yourself and those you love. One of the first things to be neglected as we get busier and busier is our sense of personal balance.

Many of us are so busy putting out fires that we forget what balance even looks like. We know we are out of balance though when the littlest of things begin to upset our entire day. When we dread doing the things that normally do not bother us or when we lose our temper easily with others. We know we are out of balance when we do not have time for any type of spontaneity or when we cannot remember the last time that we really had fun.

How do you remove feelings of being overwhelmed?

You can accomplish anything by breaking the larger goal down into smaller tasks. We like to call this chunking down.

Start with the end in mind; what does completion look like? Brainstorm the steps that will get you to your finished goal. With all of your goals and large projects make them manageable by writing down all of the tasks that may need to be completed. Keep brainstorming until you have everything written down. Do not worry about order.

When this step is completed you can organize your tasks into a general timeline or enter them and prioritize them in your to do list application software. Then do the task that seems logical to do first. Do not worry about doing anything else until that task is completed.

When you are finished then go to the next task. As you are working on your project you will find lots of other tasks to be completed. Put these in your timeline or in your to do list application software and keep moving forward.

Imagine taking a large goal such as writing a book in thirty days. This could easily cause you to become overwhelmed. You may not know where to start.

However, all you need to do is "stop" take some deep breaths and realize you do know what to do; you just need to take it step by step. Do not worry about how to do everything, just focus on the first step.

An ancient Chinese proverb says, "A journey of a thousand miles begins with a single step."

If you have difficulties along the way or cannot imagine the tasks needed to be successful then find someone who has done what you want to accomplish. See if they will mentor or coach you. Our favorite place to find help is with mastermind groups also known as professional roundtables. You can also read a book or take a course that may place you in the right direction. Another way to find help is to type in "how to..." in Google.

When you break down your goals into smaller, daily tasks it is easier to accomplish them. You are not thinking that you have to do these same things tomorrow or every day for the next four months. You are focused only on the day ahead of you. Tell yourself that just for today you are going to reach out to a new potential client, make that phone call or speak to a local organization.

As mentioned before an important factor to eliminating overwhelming feelings is to find balance in your life. Finding balance requires you to stop making excuses and start taking care of yourself. Plan your day, get a little exercise, find some time each day to be quiet and eat nutritious foods.

If you do not include these things in your daily routine, you will eventually "burn out" and your success will be derailed as well. Remember, you do not have to do everything perfectly and small bites size chunks take you a long way.

Time away from work also does wonders for your soul and helps you find balance in your life. Schedule regular time-outs away from anything work related. You will feel more energized and you will get your creative juices flowing again.

What are some action steps you can take?

Take each goal and brainstorm tasks that need to be done.

Find a mastermind group to brainstorm and strategize or join Holistic Marketing Mentors mastermind groups.

Find a mentor or coach to help you see not only the big picture but also the small steps that need to be accomplished.

Work on keeping balance in your life.

Plan time for exercise, meditation, eating right and even schedule a vacation.

Additional Resources

Being in Balance by Wayne Dyer
www.holisticmarketingmentors.com/consulting - Coaching and mentoring
www.holisticmarketingmentors.com/mastermindgroup - Mastermind group
www.getitdoneapp.com - To do lists
www.createspace.com – Self publisher for print books
www.kdp.amazon.com- Self publisher for Kindle books
www.smashwords.com – Self publisher for all e-books
www.audible.com – Self publisher for audio books

SELF MASTERY TIP #7

YOU, Everyday Self Care

Why do people put themselves last on the list? There are a number of answers to this question but for wellness professionals one of the reasons is because they love helping other people.

Every day you see clients that having been putting themselves last and the consequences it causes yet you are probably doing the same thing.

Years ago, it might have been noble to be busy 24/7, helping the kids, neighbors, relatives, etc. However, in today's world, in the new age of consciousness taking care of you is slowly becoming more acceptable. More importantly, it is a necessary ingredient for your success as a wellness professional. How many clients do you think you will have and retain if you look sick, tired and run down?

This sounds so obvious yet few of us really get it and apply it in our life. There are a few steps in this process.

How do you start to take care of you and actions steps you can take?

First, make a list of everything you take care of during a day, week, and year. Recognize where you are putting yourself on this list.

Second, look at your list and see what things you can eliminate. Many times staying busy has become a habit. Slow down; look at what is no longer serving you and your needs. Perhaps you are doing something out of obligation or guilt. Take time to evaluate each of your "so called" obligations and activities.

Make a list of "me time" things you can do.

Schedule in your calendar "me time" every day. It could be as little as 10 minutes; gradually build up this time.

Be sure to exercise regularly and healthy.

Take time to plan your meals.

Schedule regular days off or vacations to refresh and revitalize your spirit.

> *Traci's Story – I am a true high achiever. I want to accomplish everything and in addition, I want to be*

the best at everything I do. Because of these traits, it is very easy to put myself last and just go, go, go.

I know that if I do this and do not take care of myself, I will not be able to accomplish anything. I have interviewed so many people as co-founder of World Wellness Education and they have shown me through their stories the importance of self care. They have taught me that if I do not take care of myself with exercise, nutrition, sleep, meditation and relaxation than I will find myself riddled with dis-ease. When this happens, we are forced to stop and take care of ourselves and at that time, nothing else matters. Without our health, our accomplishments become secondary.

I am thankful that I have these reminders around me constantly so that I make sure that I get my exercise in five to six days a week, I eat nutritiously and I meditate regularly. I take the time to journal and relieve the stress in my life. I enjoy time with my family and I look for ways I can have fun that are not goal oriented. I have learned that I can still do everything and have everything, just not all at the same time. It is much more important to enjoy the present moment and live with minimum stress than to accomplish everything at once and enjoy none of it.

Additional resources

www.wholesomeresources.com – Meditation and stress reduction

ABOUT

GAIL SOPHIA EDGELL

I have always loved health and wellness. In fact, when I was in college I was one of very few women who spent hours in the free weight area of the fitness center. As I continued to study Exercise Physiology, I immersed myself even deeper into the wellness field. Over the years, I even was an amateur boxer and fitness competitor.

In the last twenty years, I have implemented hundreds of corporate wellness initiatives in Fortune 500 companies and started the largest personal training and corporate wellness consulting practice in my county over 12 years ago. Today, I am the owner of 360Menopause.com and co-host of the 'Magnificent Menopause and Beyond' Blog Talk Radio show. I am also the co-author of the menopause book series, *What the Hell is Happening to Me?* and most recently the co-author of this book, *Mastering Your Wellness Business*.

With all this experience, one thing remains very evident to me. Consumers are not being given all of their options. One of the reasons why this is occurring is because the alternative and integrative medicine worlds are not getting the exposure they need for it to be on the forefront of consumer minds.

That is exactly why Traci and I started our newest venture, which serves you, the professional. We believe alternative medicine and conventional medicine will integrate in less than 10 years. We want to assist you in building strong practices through business skills development, mindset and exposure.

I am dedicated to helping you change this world.

TRACI BROSMAN

Like Gail, I have always been drawn to the alternative health industry. Growing up near Seattle, Washington allowed me to explore this industry when most people still had no idea what it was. I loved learning but knew that I was not meant to be the actual healer.

I was fascinated with the mind and how it worked. I loved the fact that with little shifts in our perception we could make dramatic shifts in our outcomes. I have studied the mind for over twenty years and what role it plays in our success and happiness. I love being able to assist our clients and see them blow past perceived barriers and reach goals that were once just dreams.

Today, I know why this has always been a passion for me and that I was right – I am not destined to be the healer – I am destined to help the healers find their individual power so that they can help even more people.

Through my involvement with World Wellness Education, I have been able to use my knowledge and skills as a speaker, author and television/radio host to share peoples healing journeys with others. I believe this is important because not only do people find hope in these stories but we often connect individuals with holistic practitioners that they may not have found otherwise.

Holistic Marketing Mentors is a wonderful vehicle where Gail and I get to share our experience and skills with others through systems that walk the holistic practitioner, personal trainer, nutritionist and other wellness professionals through creating a successful business from the ground up. Our programs are designed with your success in mind. Everything we do is built around this goal!

Made in the USA
Charleston, SC
11 January 2013